RESISTING TRUMP—TEACHING ENGLISH LANGUAGE ARTS IN THE AGE OF THE DEMAGOGUE

Laurence and Mike Peters

Chapters

Introduction: The Need for Critical Pedagogy	1
Chapter One : Trump's Rhetorical Road to Power	12
Chapter Two: George Orwell's 1984 and the Rise of the Authoritarian Mindset	28
Chapter Three: Fahrenheit 451 and the Rise of Anti-Intellectualism	39
Chapter Four: Hunger Games: The Arts of Resistance	54
Chapter Five: The Bluest Eye: Resisting Trump's Racist Appeals	64
Chapter Six: Trump and Shakespeare	76
Chapter Seven: Framing Trump	90
Conclusion	98
Further Reading	100
Appendix	102

© Changingtimespress 2017

Introduction

As we endure the first months of the Trump administration, a key but very uncomfortable question keeps arising. What do we say to our children about the current occupant of the White House and the most powerful office holder in the world? What are our students in particular to make of a commander in chief who sends out bellicose tweets on a regular basis that may end up taunting his nuclear armed adversaries like North Korea into war? What do we make of the fact that a four time bankrupt has no guilt about the many contractors he stiffed, who lies regularly about big and small things, who set up a get rich quick scheme to milk retired people of their savings and who is also a serial womanizer. As educators do we sit back and watch the spectacle or do we in some shape or form decide to enter the highly controversial political fray? Can we allow our students now coming to maturity in the age of Trump as the new normal rather than the aberration he most certainly is. Is there a danger that Trump's erratic bullying absurdly narcissistic behavior is seen as the way powerful leaders need to behave and that those who don't conform to this nasty profile will be deemed as weaklings or failures to employ elements of Trump's Darwinian world-view.

Trump`s positions on everything, from the rights of minorities, immigrants and refugees, to his Darwinian view of society – a view that would allow those without means to be denied health care and continues to give tax breaks and privileges to the top one percent. Whose casual way with facts, and lack of respect for the truth and for reasoned argument sends a signal that such basic enlightenment values as tolerance, fairness and freedom – values that have been shared by generations of Americans are fungible and ultimately trivial when compared to those of someone with the reckless bravado to every day undermine these values.

The reason we wrote this book then is because, as teachers, we are very concerned about the negative Trump effect on everyone but particularly on our most impressionable, our young people. But what can we as teachers do about this? We are not supposed to be political --we are not supposed to take sides in the ongoing debate between left and right, between the GOP and the Democrats to put it more precisely. If we do, the argument goes we might endanger our employment particularly in these fractious times when political tensions are high. Point taken. But suppose we looked at the situation from another vantage point. Let's suppose that we see the Trump presidency not through partisan eyes but as a teachable moment--equivalent to say the Kennedy assassination or Nixon's resignation. In these instances, there is no escaping that people's eyes and ears are riveted to the TV coverage and that their conversation is inescapably full of the news. In both instances--even though we were residing in the UK at the time – people, no matter what their political persuasion, could not stop talking about the event, speculating as people do in times of crisis. Why did it happen? What comes next? How will this all affect such things as the price of oil, the future stability of the world, the next election? The Trump election gives us not one moment like this but because of the nature of the man and his particular path to power - it gives us multiple moments filled with crisis points.

We can take just a few:

One of his first acts in coming to office was to boast about the size of his inauguration crowd as the largest in American history despite the fact that eyewitnesses and satellite photographs showed a contrary picture. Notwithstanding the reality he sent out on his first mission his press officer, Sean Spicer to claim that "This was the largest audience ever to witness an inauguration, period, both in person and around the globe," "and then proceeded to accuse the press of "deliberately false reporting." This big lie comes after Trump's birther allegation and the news that his Trump University was nothing but a sham and a vehicle to milk retirees of their life savings. In the words of the famous phrase you cannot make this stuff up. As teachers we are given the responsibility by society to put a premium on telling the truth. We punish students who lie, even about trivial matters such as the reason why they did not attend school on a particular day, bring their homework etc. How comes then the president can seem to lie with impunity? If we don't point this out when we can find the opportunity we might be accused of neglecting our duty as good moral leaders.

We only need to remember how so many people in Germany, during the 1930s and Hitler's rise, witnessed some appalling events, that included outright lies about their country and the threats it faced as Hitler and his cabal used propaganda to take the country into war. We all are moral human beings first and then citizens and professionals. Anyone who has read anything about the German experience with Hitler's rise clearly must always come back to the age-old question--if I had been alive during that horrific period--what would I have done? If I were a teacher would I call out to some of my students what was going on? Help them to understand how their love of country was being subverted into a perverse religion? How the dehumanization of fellow human beings such as those of Jewish faith and Gypsies was just the start of a descent into barbarism in which these less than equal human beings would be sent off to gas chambers and systematically murdered? Some might react to that parallel between Hitler and Trump as too strong, even sensationalistic. But before you dismiss the comparison you need to read what the Anne Frank Center (a human rights organization named after World War II diarist Anne Frank) stated after an incident where the latter openly praised police brutality. The Center referenced the Holocaust in their cautionary note to the country, [1]

The Anne Frank Center for Mutual Respect, a New York City–based nonprofit that says it was founded by Anne's father in 1959, shared an image on Twitter of a bulleted list, laying out what appeared to be similarities between Trump and Nazi leader, Adolf Hitler. Among them were "the president creates his own media," "he endorses police brutality," and "he demonizes people who believe, look or love differently."

"Alarming parallels of history escalate," the Center wrote. Executive director, Steven Goldstein, added that it is "indeed our moral imperative, to point out parallels between actions taken by the Trump administration today and the actions taken by Germany in the 1930s before the Holocaust." Goldstein goes on to say - "1930s Germany imposed a series of escalating steps of oppression, including demonization, discrimination and isolation of vulnerable communities, that evoke what we are seeing today. That comparison is just, and not to make the comparison would be a dereliction of our duty to ensure 'never again' to any people." Author of the critically reviewed "On Tyranny" Timothy Synder argues that it is "not that Hitler is just like Trump or Trump is just like Hitler. The premise is that democratic republics usually fail and it's useful for us to see how they

---

[1] http://www.businessinsider.com/yale-professor-shouldnt-afraid-compare-trump-hitler-on-tyranny-comparison-politics-2017-4

fail. One of the ways a democratic republic can fail is Germany in 1933. There are plenty of other examples in Snyder's book, including the left-wing Czechoslovakia in 1948 becoming communist. The point of the book is that these things really happened over and over again and that intelligent people, no less intelligent than us, experienced them and left a record for us to learn from.

The question remains what to do as a teacher? Where to take a stand when Trump makes a racist speech or sends out a hateful tweet for the whole world to see. Surely, we cannot stand back as innocent bystanders? Surely, as teachers we have a duty to speak out. But how? There is a risk of alienating parents of course. So far, it should be noted, parents are more upset judging from the number of incidents reported concerning the suppression of their students' first amendment rights to be for Trump than for any remarks that teachers have made. So, for example, when one parent complained that their child's pro-Trump shirt was erased when the photo was placed into the Yearbook, the substitute teacher was dismissed and when a teacher told two of her students that wearing a T shirt with a "Make America Great Again" slogan was like wearing a swastika and that they should turn the shirts inside out, the teacher was fired after the incident went viral on social media.[2] We believe that the resistance to Trump need not be so crude and insulting to students' dignity and free speech rights but should be temperate and measured. We envisage discussions with students that naturally intersect around "teachable moments" that occur whenever commonly read set texts are read in today's classroom. We believe the purpose of the discussions should be developmental rather than have a political agenda.

Teaching with a Moral Purpose

Rafe Esquith, in his brilliant book, *Teach like your Hair's on Fire* refers to six levels of Moral Development. They are ways to move your students towards a more developed moral conscience – one that goes beyond doing something just because you don't want to get into trouble or to please somebody to motivations – level 5 and 6 - that are based on the ability to show empathy with others and a code of personal behaviour. Esquith makes the concept of empathy very concrete -- "Just imagine a world of Level V thinkers. We'd never again have to listen to the idiot barking into his cell phone. No one would cut us off when we're driving or in line for a movie. Noisy neighbors would never disturb our sleep in a hotel at 2:00 am." After battling away at trying to get the ideas across

---

[2] https://www.nytimes.com/2017/06/12/nyregion/trump-yearbook-suspended.html
http://www.okayplayer.com/culture/georgia-teacher-fired-comparing-trump-maga-shirts-swastikas.html

to his students, Esquith returns to one of his favorite novels, *To Kill a Mockingbird* to illustrate empathy and the section where Atticus gives his daughter Scout a piece of advice, "You never really understand a person until you consider things from his point of view, .until you climb inside his skin and walk around in it."

For level 6, he refers to the example of Gary Cooper's character in *High Noon*-the gunmen are ready to kill the upstanding sheriff and the inhabitants of the frightened town have all left. He remains despite the odds that he will be killed because upholding the law defines who he is as a man. With a gifted teacher like Esquith and a class of well supported, well provided elementary and middle school students, you can do wonders helping your students move beyond the stages 1-4 and enable them to become level 5 and 6 learners.

However, it remains a challenge mostly because the society as a whole seems to be working in favor of everyone getting their piece of the pie. As economic inequality grows--many are too busy to worry about those left behind as they scramble for their own lifeboats. In addition, the rise of social media has contributed to the notion that we can just communicate with like-minded individuals Furthermore, in an era in which the curriculum is narrowing and teachers` autonomy is being challenged by the requirement to teach to standardized tests, there is less and less opportunity for teachers to address key issues of the day in ways that encourage students to become independent thinkers.

Ways Forward

There are several ways forward that depend on our willingness to take seriously that you have a responsibility to teach critical thinking as part of your subject matter--whether that subject matter include history, literature or social studies. We believe that part of the reason why students do not graduate from high school and certainly flounder in college is their lack of critical thinking skills. What do we mean by this? It means they fail to apply what they learn to concrete situations. It is as if "school knowledge" was situated at one remove from reality – that the facts and figures, dates and concepts existed in a separate world of their own, too disconnected and fragmented, for them to pull it all together to make meaningful sense.

If we had to come up with a quick definition of what critical thinking actually means it would be close to this--the ability to apply critical reasoning, empathetic and creative skills to a variety of real world situations and problems and to do so while escaping the crowd's prejudices. A common definition, according to Art Costa, a professor emeritus of education at California State University, Sacramento, is "the examination and evaluation of ideas, events and arguments in their contexts.[3] As such, it includes "questioning assumptions and identifying biases." It is the also the capacity for independent and creative "higher order thinking" and it is an area that US schools do not do very well in fostering, as the results of the PISA exam - a test specifically designed to measure critical thinking skills bears out. PISA tests a wide number of skills but they tend to be focused on applying math and literacy skills to coming up with arguments, such as which companies` literature offers the best cell phone plans. This, is of course, one key area of critical thinking and one that needs more time in the curriculum--it can be broadly captured under the term "real world problem solving" but to us, it is of secondary importance to the class of civic-minded thinking focused on the social and moral issues that Esquith is concerned with.

The term "civics" is used with some deliberation. Now out of fashion as a separate subject in many schools, it has been nudged aside by STEM subjects that focus on the employment skills schools believe they should teach rather than the skills required for students to participate in a vibrant democracy as thoughtful citizens. One indication of the damage neglect of civics education can do is revealed by a 2015 study conducted by the Annenberg Public Policy Center at the University of Pennsylvania, which showed that only 31% of Americans can name the three branches of government (and 32% cannot name a single branch). In 2011, when Newsweek administered the United States Citizenship Test to over 1000 American citizens, 38% of Americans failed. [4]

But where to find the time and the room in the curriculum to do any of this citizenship patching work? How to begin? First there is a myth about not enough time. There is plenty of wasted time in the class day. Most of the busy work we get our students to do is not productive--we all know what that is--stuff we give our students to do so we can relax for a bit and get our heads together. Filling out quizzes and surveys that we will never read, coloring in shapes and repetitious tasks. Then there are the natural breaks when you finish a unit. In a 35 hour teaching day--if those gaps and

---

[3] http://library.cqpress.com/cqresearcher/document.php?id=cqresrre2015041000

[4] https://www.everyday-democracy.org/news/decline-civic-education-and-effect-our-democracy

busy work times amount to just 5 percent of the week we have just over an hour to work with, There is a lot you can do if you are organized in 60 minute or fewer chunks during the week to promote critical thinking.

We are confident that you can find ways to integrate the approaches discussed here into your teaching, whether you are an English Language Arts, History, Social Studies or general Humanities teacher in general. The key aspect of our approach that is worth noting is that it makes an effort to connect the fragmentary bits and pieces of the English Language Arts, social studies and history curriculum within unifying themes. We also believe that for ideas to "stick" to become meaningful, students need to hear ideas from multiple sources, in multiple formats and be given the opportunity to explore the thoughts using a multiple number of formats, not just the typically given factual quiz and essay.

They also need to wrap their imaginations around the idea of why, for example, equal justice for all or freedom of speech are such vital ideas by role playing scenarios involving the suppression of human rights those around the world who have been denied equal justice or freedom of speech, by writing their own poems and stories and even making their own videos. . To use the modern lingo, students need to connect their left brain feeling and imaginative centers to their right brain analytical and thinking processes. We believe this missing connection, when it comes to the curriculum today, is highly relevant to the ability to really develop critical thinkers capable of problem solving in an ethical and humane way.

Students need not just to connect the various fragments of knowledge that can be culled from the disconnected curriculum but to be able to see that knowledge as having relevance in their own lives. To achieve this goal, teachers need to move away from the way the conventional curriculum operates--teacher and textbook centered instruction, providing little or no rationale as to how the topic connects with other topics or is relevant to students` lives. Critical pedagogy starts form the notion that students are not passive learners, without agency, prior knowledge or individual concerns or needs. Freire, who so aptly characterized the approach of handing out and checking bits of information, as the "banking system" and who can be said to have founded critical pedagogy, proposes instead a problem-based learning, where students enter into a dialogue with their teachers, unrestrained by grades and the usual ways teachers impose authority and subordination on their students.

Although Freire's approach sounds fine and logical progressive and all the other positive words we can bestow on an idea, the kind of two- way dialogue that he proposes is too little practiced in schools. The pressures on teachers to play the authoritarian role are for many too much to resist. We are all fearful as teachers about giving up power to students--what if they take advantage--find a weakness and exploit it? It is also hard intellectual work--it forces us, as well as the students, to think for themselves. So why do it? Why risk our authority and why do we need to place extra demands on ourselves? We believe that the reason is that the times demand a change. We cannot keep turning out students, who have so very little clue about the world--who might be tempted for a second Trump term--in four years (as of this time of writing, the 14 year olds we now teach will be eligible to vote). Clearly, they have a right to vote for who they want--but they need to know what Trump stands for --in more depth than they are offered in the sound -bite age that we live in.

Classroom Approaches

So, what is our approach--our recipe for helping our students resist Trump's appeal? We recommend a multiple number of approaches that are designed to get students to think for themselves. One of the techniques is to try old fashioned discussion that is focused around problem solving. A particular problem facing the world--for example—is climate change.

The discussion might go like this:

1. You present an article from a newspaper that indicates that climate change is a growing problem as exemplified by the melting of the polar ice caps or the flooding experienced by some low- lying islands in the southern hemisphere. Your next move is to have the students read the article or view the news clip and ask them what have they learned so far if anything about the problem (bringing into play their past knowledge) and how this news clip fits into their understanding of the issue.

2. You then ask how should we solve the problem of climate change? You should then work your way to a question--we cannot solve it without understanding some causal factors. The discussion might include how do they determine what are relevant sources. Hopefully the discussion includes that these sources must have some kind of scientific validity and must be verifiable by data and experimentation.

3. We then ask what are the areas of consensus and who disagrees and why?

4. This is where we can discuss the Trump's administration's extreme views that deny climate change. However, instead of just calling him out we can discuss what are the arguments he puts forward--he has variously called global warming a "hoax," and as a campaigner he stated he was "not a big believer in man-made climate change," and also suggested that "nobody really knows" if climate change exists. We then ask whether these views are consistent with the evidence and then if not why he might put those views forward. Who benefits from climate denial? Do any of his billionaire backers for example?

5. Is Trump one of a kind or have we seen any of this behavior before--denial of science and reason to advance a particular interest? We can refer to *1984*-- here is a whole state dedicated to denial of reality not just science--they want to wage a war even against the proposition that 2+2=4. All thought is subjected to the power of the totalitarian big brother.

Is that then the end of it? By no means--we have just started down the path towards critical thinking. We might go several ways, depending on you, the teacher and the group/s you are working with, following one of several issues for which there are no clear answers. So, if the climate change discussion went well and the students are now curious as to how someone in power can baldly deny the scientific consensus you can engage them with some discussions that require them to go a bit deeper. For example, we can ask whether Trump's denial of facts is because he does not have the mental capacity to understand them? Or does he do it because he knows that his rich backers benefit? This then gets into a discussion of power--we can ask the following questions -

1. Does power corrupt? If so why and how?
2. What are the effective ways to resist corruption and abuse of power?

3. Is Trump typical American leader or do we need to look around the world and in history for his forebears to see how this attitude to facts ends up?

Another approach would be to move from the more general ways that Trump's approaches to the world--with respect, for example, to the perceived dangers posed by illegal immigrants, Muslims or links up to better understanding the techniques he uses to get his audience to accept non-scientific explanations that satisfy his desire to simplify problems. These techniques include -

1. Binary thinking--forcing people to choose between "us and them" when the choices are far more complex

2. Single narrative explanations.

3. Conspiracy theories

In the book we give examples of how all three types of lazy thinking are very easy for people to swallow and are very common tools used by the totalitarian thinkers throughout history.

Another approach which depends on getting students to appreciate the power of the arts (whether they be in the form of novels, short stories, plays, poems, songs) to help us understand the way abstract concepts like power, totalitarian thinking work in the real world. In fact it is our strong belief that although discussion and argument of the kind described above can get us far down the road to enabling students to develop a fuller way to counter the mindsets that might lead to a Trump vote, we need to provide a fuller human context that only the arts can supply as to why the Trump view of the world is so wrong-headed, so lacking not just in logic but in basic humanity that it needs to be rejected.

However, how do you fit that dimension into your 60 minute time period you feel is reasonable to allocate over a week? This is where we need to rely on some ingenuity as well as some assistance from technology in the form of YouTube. In this day and age, we cannot naively pin our hopes on our students suddenly wanting to pick up and read a book that is outside of the curriculum reading. We need to recognize our real role today is to stimulate a desire to read and to curate that reading experience. So that is why in the thematic part of the book we are recommending audio or film clips of recommended books being performed. We provide a list of these YouTube videos as starting points for the discussion and they serve the added benefit that they can be watched in 5 or 10 minute segments by the students before, during or after the "lesson" and so the 15 or 20 minutes you have free can be used for the discussion.

After an introduction to critical pedagogy that will highlight why it is so key to confronting the Trump mindset, the book is organized into themes. The themes are first discussed in anchor texts. We provide short summaries, trailers if you like, that highlight the ways the book's theme is explored through characters and action and the key issues that only great art and literature can bring to life. In other words, we do not neatly bundle these summaries into a nicely wrapped short story--we expose the questions that the author was wrestling with. These "trailer summaries' are designed to get the students to read the book or if that is not the next step they take to see a clip from the movie of the book and/or a movie that explores a related idea. We then pose discussion questions that can be handled in a 5-20 minute exchange depending on how deep you want to go.

Our next step is to help you springboard from the discussion about the anchor text to two relevant historical periods--one that relates to world the other related to US history. Again where appropriate, relevant YouTube videos are identified but again as with the trailer summaries that we use to get the students' excited by reading a book--we provide a trailer for the particular historical period and again expose the questions that this episode in history reveals about the theme. As a follow up, we provide a menu of ways to now start applying the themes discussed in the anchor text and the relevant historical periods to their own lives. Students can choose to tell the story or episode from a different perspective. For example, Watergate might be told from the point of view of a soldier who feels disappointed in his government after he sacrificed a limb in Viet Nam or Hamlet told from Ophelia's point of view. They should be able to choose to write this as a straightforward story, poem or graphic novel.

A third section is designed to help your students spot the techniques that manipulators use (mostly politicians and business people) to use emotional or other appeals to close down critical thinking. We classify them as Framing the Argument

Chapter One: Trump's Rhetorical Road to Power

Those of us interested in the future of democracy and feel it is under threat by Trump, might want to include a lesson or two about how he won the 2016 election. But how can we do this so the lesson does not look like we are partisan, intolerant and simply anti-Trump, or determined to force feed our students with a one-sided political ideology? The answer is that is possible to smoothly integrate a neutral strategy, as long as we focus on the relevant standards points.

All teachers are in some way or another English teachers, so you virtually have a blanket license to adopt the 8th grade English Language Arts Common Core Standards (CCSS.ELA-LITERACY.SL.8.2) which calls for students to be able to "Analyze the purpose of information presented in diverse media and formats (e.g., visually, quantitatively, orally). Additionally, CCSS.ELA-LITERACY.SL.8.3. Additionally, students are expected to "delineate a speaker's argument and specific claims, evaluating the soundness of the reasoning and relevance and sufficiency of the evidence and identifying when irrelevant evidence is introduced."[5]

The Common Core standards that apply to Social Studies and History go further by recognizing "the importance of preparation for civic life." The Introduction notes that students who meet the standards are able to "reflexively demonstrate the cogent reasoning and use of evidence that is essential to both private deliberation and responsible citizenship in a democratic republic."[6] These

---

[5] http://www.corestandards.org/ELA-Literacy/SL/8/
[6] National Governors Association Center for Best Practices (NGA) and Council of Chief State School Officers (CCSSO), Common Core State Standards for English Language Arts and Literacy in History/ Social Studies,

Standards also promote inter- disciplinary approaches and the application of knowledge and concepts in real-world settings.

In light of the above, it is possible to construct lessons that address Trump 's use of language as long as we don`t solely focus in on him as the only politician who uses rhetorical devices to build a base of support. Our task should be to compare his methods with his contemporaries and to look back and forward in history and literature to compare how he uses some well-worn techniques with those of his predecessors. That way we cannot be accused of picking on Trump.

Opening Discussion

Start by asking the question--how did Trump, a virtual unknown to the political landscape use words and argument against practiced and experienced politicians to build a base of support capable of winning the presidency?

You might get the following replies--ranging from he was just better at putting his point across, to he was not a phony like the rest of them career politicians or that he was better known because of his starring role of the major hit series, *The Apprentice*. Some might say he was wealthier than all of the other politicians and so he could finance his own campaign. Others might say he was a businessman who "knew how to get things done." All of these ideas are worth discussing because they do suggest that he had some ability to stand out from the pack but they fail to get at how he used the above advantages to win. You might ask students to consider that for all of Trump's advantages, his rise was never a "slam dunk" as he was also carrying a considerable amount of baggage. In the media he has consistently been portrayed as a playboy, philanderer, a four-time bankrupt, as someone with potential mob connections and as someone who put his name to a phony "get rich scheme" known as Trump University.

As students shift their attention away from why Trump might have been successful to how Trump used the tools at his disposal to turn his unlikely background into his ultimately successful campaign to occupy the Oval Office, you might reference some other unlikely political leaders – leaders like Adolf Hitler, for example, who was an unsuccessful corporal who became Chancellor of Germany. There are some surprising comparisons to be drawn between both career paths as we shall see but it is clearly a professional judgement on how much we want to stress any of them.

Science, and Technical Subjects (Washington, D.C.: NGA and CCSSO, 2010

What is clearly also interesting to note is that all leaders --whether they be Trump, Nixon, Kennedy or Churchill – use techniques of persuasion that date back to the Greeks and if anyone is interested in researching those there is a reading list at the end.

Here, are a number of the well-known tools, Trump used to help overcome some of the serious hurdles to his candidacy.

Tools of Persuasion

First Challenge --How does a billionaire who travels around in his own gold plated 747 get to represent the hoi polloi and begin to offer himself as their mouthpiece?

Answer: He gets to inhabit their attitudes to the powerful and he uses their language and conversational style and attitudes to express solidarity.

Pretending to be Like You

Trump understood the electoral value of pretending to share with a huge swathe of disaffected voters, particularly those located in the south and mid-west of the country (what elites have sometimes dismissively referenced as "flyover country") their feeling of powerlessness – a powerlessness due to the decline of their income and the ravaging of their communities by unemployment, drug addiction and a host of other modern ills. Trump was able to persuade this group of disaffected voters (even though he had voted against the economic bailout for the auto industry that came hard upon the 2004 recession) that that he, unlike the perceived elites, cared about their economic futures. He did this by directing their anger against the trade agreements that he blamed the Clinton for, which he contended had lost jobs to Mexico. He directed their anger at Hillary, and her former president husband Bill, who were, he argued, the ones that had caused the mess they were in and he was about to reverse course on these trade agreements.

To effectively channel the anger of the disaffected he had to do the following:

Tell the Victim Story

The victim story is one of the best stories for gaining power there is. Why? It has a villain and a savior - two necessary people to make any story work. It also has the benefit of helping the audience understand that they are the subject of an abuse or a crime that others have been complicit in covering up. It also, when told well, allows the speaker to be identified as the audience's friend and champion. The use of victimhood as a path to power was a tactic Hitler used when he accused those who had signed the Versailles treaty as selling out the country and blaming international bankers and Jews for conspiring against German interests and thus causing a massive depression and famine in some parts of the country.

Trump's path was to single out the trade agreements negotiated by Bill Clinton and later his wife (NAFTA and TPP) as the reason why there was so much unemployment in the rust belt and why average standards of living had either stagnated or had fallen back. In doing so he came close to demonizing Hillary Clinton, calling her "Crooked Hillary" and leading chants for her to be locked up for her use of a separate server. When you tell a victim story, you have to repeat it over and over again for the ideas to sink into the public. Trump did this repeatedly at his rallies as well as praising the audience in lines such as - "We're going to make America strong again — like the people that are here — strong people."

Tell Big Lies

Of course, this victim story is dependent on the telling of some big lies--that Hillary Clinton did negotiate the NAFTA treaty (she did not - her husband did and she called for TPP to be renegotiated) and that it was responsible for huge job losses in the mid-west which was not the case. Other `whoppers` Trump told included saying that Obama was not an American citizen but was born in Kenya and that was the reason he could not produce the long form of his birth certificate.

Hitler was the one who first used the big lie and employed the following rather intricate reasoning to justify it, "that in the big lie there is always a certain force of credibility; because the broad masses of a nation are always more easily corrupted in the deeper strata of their emotional nature than consciously or voluntarily; and thus in the primitive simplicity of their minds they more readily fall victims to the big lie than the small lie, since they themselves often tell small lies in little matters but would be ashamed to resort to large-scale falsehoods. It would never come into their heads to fabricate colossal untruths, and they would not believe that others could have the impudence to distort the truth so infamously. Even though the facts which prove this to be so may be brought clearly to their minds, they will still doubt and waver and will continue to think that there may be some other explanation. For the grossly impudent lie always leaves traces behind it, even after it has been nailed down, a fact which is known to all expert liars in this world and to all who conspire together in the art of lying. (Adolf Hitler, Mein Kampf, vol. I, ch. X[1])

The key phrase there is "leave traces behind it" --even after the lie is disproved it still works its ugly magic on the brain. The point of the birther big lie then was not to force Obama out of office as someone who had lied on his employment application forms but to give legitimacy to those who doubted he was truly an American. To cast doubt on his nationality was a small step to casting doubt on his legitimacy as a president.

Trump came out with some other big lies during the campaign. He claimed for example that "Obama, aided and abetted by Hillary Clinton, founded the Islamic State." Repeating according to the Miami Herald, "the phony charge nearly 20 times over the following two days until he finally had to walk it back as "sarcasm." But then he even amended that by saying, "well, really not so much."[7]Trump succeeded in painting a dark view of America and the world. He painted the choice between himself and Hilary in bleak terms. Hillary Clinton's only economic plan was to "offer a welfare check". She had, according to Trump, to all intents and purposes, abandoned ordinary Americans by calling them "deplorables". He can then present himself as their savior running on behalf of "the forgotten men and women of America. People who work hard but don't have a voice. I am running to be their voice, and to fight to bring prosperity to every part of this country." Trump, of course, was going to be their voice after appointing as many former Goldman Sachs bankers and fellow billionaires as he could find to stuff his cabinet with.

Use Repetition and Emotion to Gain Solidarity by Demonizing the Other

---

[7] http://www.miamiherald.com/opinion/op-ed/article96105412.html

All of Trump's techniques depend on his ability to trigger the emotional centers of your brain so they will overwhelm the rational and sensible sides of them. It is no accident that Trump found his stride when he addressed massive rallies of thousands of people, who he was able to wind up into a frenzied screaming mass of supporters. As one observer at his rallies remarked, "I've seen politicians cast a spell over an audience before, but none like Donald Trump. The rally had a kind of religious fervor. But of a toxic variety. The arena — packed with perhaps 10,000 people — was ripe with vitriol. I've never seen so many angry, middle-aged-to-elderly white people at a political event." The anger had to be channeled against perceived enemies that were opposed to "making America Great Again." Muslims were on that list as were journalists who arrived there by reporting the truth about Trump - a truth that Trump wanted the audience to reject as "fake news" and as either unfair or dishonest.

However, the worst people were protesters. Trump masterfully turned all of his irrational hatred of truth and opposition to his advantage as the stadium rallies were transformed into a potent kind of political theatre that gave permission to his supporters to use hate as a way of intensifying their support of their leader, much as Hitler was able to do in the famous Nuremberg rallies, where groups of true believers were incited to beat up protesters.

According to <u>Scientific American report,</u> a message was broadcast over the PA system "not to touch any protesters they spotted. Rather they were told to notify security by chanting, "Trump! Trump! Trump! ...What occurred next were plenty of false alarms that resulted in repeated chanting that served to unite the crowd against perceived enemies in their midst. It was the first among many efforts to see any form of dissent and argument as hostile to their group solidarity."

The next move was to enclose the media in their own pen--like a cattle enclosure so that they could be used as exhibit number one in Trump's tirade against what he saw was the liberal fake media that was viewed as hostile to his point of view. Trump had no compunction in leading a chorus of hate against them, referring to them as "the most disgusting" and "the most dishonest people he's ever seen", causing the crowd to turn their hatred and boos in their direction and feel powerful when they did so because now Trump had given them a voice to talk back to an institution that they were encouraged to see as a faceless elite that was unconcerned with their interests. .

Create a Straw Man

Trump did not want to engage in policy or in detail. He was much more comfortable in using a substitute for policy analysis, namely to create a straw man argument, a fictional argument and a fictional opponent that are far easier to knock down and dismiss than the real thing. The tactic is based on deliberate misrepresentation of the other side's argument and is, in reality, a close cousin of the big lie. Trump wanted NRA support and so was prepared to use perhaps the most fanatical group of people in the country to rally to his side. All he had to do to attract that support was to exaggerate and lie about Clinton's position on guns, which was that while she respected the Second Amendment, she was in favor of more regulation of handguns. As he said in one rally, "Hillary Clinton wants to take your guns away, and she wants to abolish the Second Amendment!" If you are Hillary Clinton all you can do is to defend your position, which is not nearly as headline-worthy or media worthy as the neatly packaged soundbite that Trump sent whizzing around the world at warp speed.

Use the 'ad hominem' argument/ to begin to dehumanize your opponents and turn them into caricatures.

On the Republican primary stage, surrounded by people who had actually been elected to office, held executive or legislative power, Trump needed to overcome his clear deficits in the realm of governing experience by demeaning his opponents by using personal smears, in other words - ad hominem attacks. He notably referred to Senator Marco Rubio as "Little Marco," Senator Ted Cruz as "lying Ted" and called Governor Jeb Bush, "low energy." He further made disparaging remarks about Carly Fiorina's face. [8] Trump also enjoyed referring to Hillary Clinton as "Crooked" which he continued to do multiple times the same trace impression as the birther lie--that sense that she was ineradicably corrupt and illegitimately striving for the nation's highest office. This tag led directly to the horrific "lock her up" chants that became a regular part of the rallies—unifying the crowd in more than a few minutes of hate directed at the most qualified presidential candidate in recent history.

---

[8]. "Look at that face!" Trump said about rival candidate Carly Fiorina in an interview with Rolling Stone in September 2015. "Can you imagine that, the face of our next president?! I mean, she's a woman, and I'm not s'posed to say bad things, but really, folks, come on. Are we serious?"

The target of an ad hominem attack is the person you're arguing against, rather than their ideas and one of its purposes is to slightly dehumanize them. What Trump knows is that once the term sticks, you cannot undo its effect – it becomes part of the mental furniture, the way you begin to look at the candidate. Thus, Trump found yet another way to use emotions to overwhelm the rational side of your brain. For some reason none of his rivals could make any moniker on Trump stick.

You can discuss with your class why that was. The use of a derogatory name was, of course, the first step to dismissing them as individuals worthy of standing on the same stage as the almighty Donald, the dispenser of insults. However, it was an important first step because it allowed him anytime to answer a policy question with some kind of personal jibe or attack. Part of his opponents` dignity as public officials was therefore eroded and part of Trump`s credibility as a man in the street truth-teller was elevated.

Use the Appeal to Fear Story

In conjunction with the victim story, there is the fear story and they work hand in hand. Trump wants the emotional reaction first and foremost from his audience. That is what increases their adrenaline as well as his own - the kind of adrenaline that will translate into numbers turning out on a cold November night to punch the button for his candidacy. But he knows as well, that talk of bad trade deals, even ones negotiated by his hated rival, will not generate as much heat and hatred as he needs to fuel his long-shot candidacy--he needs real fear to push his numbers up.

Trump is able to produce fear by constructing the imminent threat narrative. Since no-one has a credible nuclear threat pointed at us--the kind of fear that a Nixon or a Goldwater could generate with a not so subtle reference to the capability of Soviet Russian weapons directed to us from Cuba, he is left with the unlikely threat from across our southern border of thousands of immigrants – and not just any kind of immigrants but criminals who have been deliberately let out of their country to destroy our way of life. Trump starts this narrative in the first speech he gives as presidential candidate,

"When Mexico sends its people, they're not sending their best. They're not sending you. They're not sending you. They're sending people that have lots of problems, and they're bringing those problems with us. They're bringing drugs. They're bringing crime. They're rapists. And some, I assume, are good people.

As the speech advances, you realize that the picture that is being painted is not just of Mexican rapists that are illegally entering our unsafe borders, the threat is also from terrorists -

"It's coming from more than Mexico. It's coming from all over South and Latin America, and it's coming probably— probably— from the Middle East. But we don't know. Because we have no protection and we have no competence, we don't know what's happening. And it's got to stop and it's got to stop fast. Islamic terrorism is eating up large portions of the Middle East. They've become rich."

The message is that we are all in deep trouble--we are about to become overrun not just by people who look different from us but who want to do us harm and no one but Trump cares about the issue or can save us.. As if that is not enough fear to get you running for your safe rooms, there is more to be added to the toxic mix. As well as our borders being virtually non-existent, there is an entire religion that is organized against us,

"There is a great hatred toward Americans by a large segments of the Muslim population. It's gonna get worse and worse. You're gonna have more World Trade Centers," Trump goes on by "calling for a total and complete shutdown of Muslims entering the United States until our country's representatives can figure out what the hell is going on...We have no choice…"

Now he is playing to the country's worst fears as he sets himself up as the only person with the clear-eyed vision and macho ability to defeat these enemies. Again, Trump wants your emotional centers to overwhelm any critical processes that would, for example, suggest that only a tiny fraction of terrorists are Muslims and they are rejected by the majority and that Islam is a peaceful religion and so forth.

Use the Hidden Conspiracy Argument

Also known as the appeal to belief, the appeal to the masses, the appeal to popularity, as well as other names, the bandwagon fallacy is an argument that rests on the belief that because a lot of people agree on something, it must be correct.

This is another favorite tactic Donald Trump uses during his rallies. "I only wish these cameras — because there is nothing as dishonest as the media, that I can tell you," he has said. "I only wish these cameras would spin around and show the kind of people that we have here. The numbers of people that we have. I just wish they'd for once do it."

His boastful argument is meant to suggest that because a lot of people come out to support him at his rallies, or that because he has a lot of Twitter followers, he would be the best president. In truth, while the size of his audiences may (or may not) be a decent predictor of whether he'll receive a lot of votes, his popularity doesn't mean that his policy proposals would be any more effective than his opponent's.

Similarly, Trump has a tendency to appeal to authority (another logical fallacy) in citing his endorsements (such as those of religious leaders, basketball coaches, boxing promoters, and just broadly "many people"), to tie into the bandwagon argument, suggesting that if certain other people support Trump, you should too.

Use the False Choices Argument

The world is filled with possibilities — that is, until you deploy the black and white fallacy in an argument - also known as the false dilemma, the false dichotomy, the false choice, or bifurcation - the black and white fallacy presents situations as only having two distinct options, when in actuality there are numerous possible outcomes.

"We're going to start winning so much that you're going to get used to winning instead of getting used to losing," Trump said in a campaign video.

In this situation, the listener is being given two options: winning or losing. This quote was delivered in the context of trade deals but has been used throughout Trump's campaign to contrast himself (a winner) with his opponents (losers). Now, of course, elections have winners and losers, but Trump was speaking in a more general sense that doesn't necessarily support his argument.

Use the Genetic Fallacy Argument.

Also known as the fallacy of virtue or fallacy of origins, the genetic fallacy is an argument based on someone or something's origin, history or source. Similar to the composition fallacy, that falsely argues that because some portion of a group can be characterised in one way, all members of that group can be characterised that way. The genetic fallacy argument relies on irrelevant stereotypes.

In June 2016, Trump went on CNN to defend statements he had made about Gonzalo Curiel, a judge who was overseeing a lawsuit brought against Trump University.

"I have had horrible rulings," Trump said, arguing for Judge Curiel to recuse himself. "I have been treated very unfairly by this judge. This judge is of Mexican heritage. I'm building a wall, OK?"

Here, Trump used the genetic fallacy argument to suggest that, because Judge Curiel (who was born in Indiana, for what it's worth) is "of Mexican heritage," he can't objectively rule in any case Trump is involved in due to Trump's plans to build a wall along the U.S./Mexico border.

Use the Argument from Anecdote

Stories are great, and when used correctly, in the course of making an argument, they can be the key to persuasion. When used in lieu of hard data, however, anecdotes lose their luster.

To be sure, Donald Trump isn't the only politician to regularly rely on the use of anecdotes to make his points. Where Trump differs, however, is in how he deploys them - often without any data to back up his claim, using phrases like "many people are saying."

Claims like "Many people are now saying I won South Carolina because of the last debate," "I beat China all the time," and "I will be the best by far in fighting terror" aren't rooted in data, but rather in Trump's own feelings.

In many of Trump's anecdotes, he combines fallacies, sometimes incorporating bandwagon thinking ("Many people are saying...") or black and white arguments ("I beat China" implies there is a winner and loser in each trade deal — but there doesn't have to be! International trade doesn't need to be a zero-sum game! — and that if Trump isn't elected, we'll "lose" to China).

Trump's appeal has always been to the non-college educated working class voters. Trump has made no apologies for "loving" the "poorly educated voter." It is an uncomfortable truth that those who favor right wing parties whether they be in France (National Front), the Netherlands (Freedom Party) and Germany (Alternative for Germany) or the UK (UKIP) are predominantly those who have not advanced beyond high school. You might begin your discussion on Bradbury's *Fahrenheit 451*, after reading *1984* or after a particularly egregious Trumpian anti-intellectual act, such as taking down a government site on Climate Change or cutting off medical or scientific research funds for an agency like NIH with one of two questions

1) Why do you think Trump cut funding etc for this program? (if there is a topical fit)

Or more conventionally,

2) What do the two books, *1984* and *Fahrenheit 451* have in common?

To answer the first question students might say that Trump is not that bright and does not want to spend money on stuff he does not understand or he is opposed to like climate change.

It might be worth a quick review of what Trump has done since he has been in office to wage war against science

- In his first budget proposal he slashed EPA's funding by 31 percent, the Centers for Disease Control and Prevention's funding by 17 percent, the National Science Foundation's funding by 11 percent, and the Department of the Interior's funding by nearly 12 percent.

- Trump selected clearly unqualified candidates as heads of top scientific agencies. Instead of people like the Nobel Prize-winning physicist Steve Chu to head the Department of Energy,

Trump appointed a TV Dancing with the Stars contestant, who reportedly got Cs and Ds in physics and chemistry to oversee the nation's nuclear arsenal

- The Environmental Protection Agency removed a page that explained the causes and effects of climate change from its website

- The Interior Department's Twitter account was suspended for Tweeting out pictures, comparing President Obama's 2009 Inauguration crowd to President Trump's much smaller turnout .and created the unforgettable phrase "alternative facts"

As *Time* magazine has pointed out -

"Even before the election, Trump was a shameless peddler of scientific fictions — that climate change is a Chinese hoax; that vaccines cause autism. No sooner had he won than he conspicuously

What has this to do with us --that we have a president who can back out of the Paris Climate change agreement and can believe he knows more than experts on any given issue?

How can you engage your class in a discussion on this matter? One way into the conversation is to engage them with the question-- how did of the most educated nations in the history of the world, with more postgraduate degrees than anywhere on the planet elect such an intellectually shallow, not to say duplicitous man?

Students may need prompting so here are a few prompts:

Was the Media To Blame?

Was it the media's lack of scrutiny? As many in the media will admit, few reporters asked the hard questions that should have been asked of the candidate. There were only a handful of questions that tried to pick apart Trump's lies and evasions.. As the NPR reported "much of the political press treated Trump's campaign as pure spectacle"[9] The left-leaning Huffington Post relegated the Trump coverage during the campaign to its Entertainment section. As David Folkenflik commented, the TV interviews were often "sycophantic" affairs in which " anchors seemed somewhat giddy to interview Trump. He talked over questioners, talked past them, talked through them. On the rare occasion, one might drill down and catch him off guard. They quickly understood that Trump's rallies where he would often say or do something sensational and unscripted were a ratings gold mine as billions of dollars in free air time were given over to the Trump campaign. "It may not be good for America, but it's good for CBS," said CBS Chairman Les Moonves.

The media framed Trump as an entertaining figure with a disruptive message for the political elites that fitted perfectly his narrative that he was not a conventional politician. So instead of closely scrutinizing the scores of lawsuits that Trump has had to defend over the years, his ties to the mob, the multiple sexual harassment cases against him etc., the media preferred to show video of Trump getting off his personal 737 jet and moving towards his limo as if he were indeed the next president of the United States. The media was comfortable with a narrative they had collaborated with Trump in helping to create. Insert

Was Modern American Culture to Blame ?

The US, with its fascination with celebrity, rich people, rock stars and ratings, with its belief in winners and losers, is, of course, partly responsible for Trump. Trump could only occur in America. Only in the US can a billionaire be taken seriously as the voice of an oppressed white working-class "silent majority." We might trace this bizarre concept back to America's founding where there was a basic agreement that democracy meant that everyone, no matter his wealth or background, was fundamentally equal and had a right to express their views no matter what. Over time, this belief that everyone was entitled to his own belief has, in this modern era of celebrity, degenerated into a view that facts and expertise are not critical. It just matters whether the person sincerely expresses his or her views. Such an attitude encourages anti-intellectualism--a contempt for experts who would stand between an honestly held belief and its utterance. As the late Isaac Asimov, the prolific science fiction author, has written, "Anti-intellectualism has been a constant thread winding its way through our political and cultural life, nurtured by the false notion that democracy means that 'my ignorance is just as good as your knowledge.'"

---

[9] http://www.npr.org/2016/05/05/476944825/how-the-media-failed-in-covering-donald-trump

How Did Social Media Contribute to Trump's Rise?

Trump famously spoke to his supporters using his Twitter account. Trump's use of Twitter was nothing short of a brilliant move. No one since Trump had "weaponized" Twitter in quite the way to use 140 characters to promote himself and to denigrate his many enemies. With an unprecedented 32.4 million followers, he could, with no extra expense, communicate on a regular basis to a huge slice of the country and, in doing so, bypass the traditional media. Twitter represents, as many people have said, the modern-day version of the fireside chat--it was a vehicle more importantly that Trump, and not a surrogate used, so his voice seemed authentic and people believed he was directly talking to them. What better way to silence critics, to criticize the media as pedalling "fake news." He uses capitalization and exclamation points to convey emotions so that when we read the Tweets we also internally are hearing his voice

Below is just one example of the way Trump expresses

Nor does he use sophisticated vocabulary or engage in complex nuanced thinking. For Trump, as for his supporters, the world is black and white. Trump is engaged in constant battle with the media because he sees himself and likes to be seen as the victim of unfair reporting or some kind of vengeful campaign. In Trump-world he is wise, rich and secure and he is possessed of truth and facts that no one else has access to.

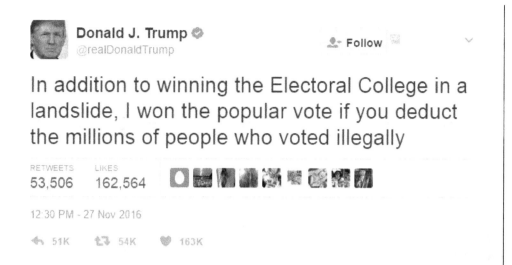

Trump's use of Twitter can enable you to talk to your class about filters and gatekeepers. It is difficult to imagine Trump storming in front of 12 seasoned professional politicians on the GOP side and his arch enemy Hillary who Trump frequently took to Twitter to vilify. In traditional campaigns, the candidates require the TV commentators to grant access and to do so they are obliged to consider balance and fairness codes, which basically means the networks (for so long just three) have to make sure that some kind of equal treatment operates with respect to candidates both in different parties and in the same party.

Trump neither needed the permission of senior media power-brokers or needed to spend millions of dollars on advertising. He could reach his core base of supporters with the touch of a finger. You might ask whether this is good or bad for democracy. Clearly there is no one right answer but in the hands of Trump, a skilled showman with little or no respect for truth or fact and with an audience who had already shown loyalty to him by accepting as a possibility his birther slander against Obama, the stage was set for Trump to go even further in weakening the idea that rationality and knowledge was a basic qualification to become president

Chapter Two: George Orwell's 1984 and the Rise of the Authoritarian Mindset

Why has Novel become a Best-Seller?

Remarkably *1984* has sold 47,000 print copies since election day in November. That is up from 36,000 copies over the same period the previous year, an increase of 30 per cent and this is on top of its bestseller status world-wide, having sold at least 30 million copies. As Peter Ross recently pointed out "the electric charge of Orwell's thinking hums and crackles through the culture." Ross noted that "almost seventy years since it was first published in 1949, the novel topped the Amazon bestseller list. Demand began to rise, according to Penguin Random House, shortly after Kellyanne Conway used the expression "alternative facts" to defend Sean Spicer's claim that Donald Trump had attracted the largest audience ever to witness a presidential inauguration, period. By July 2017 sales had doubled over the same period in 2016. Half a million copies were printed in January alone."[10]

---

[10] http://bostonreview.net/literature-culture/peter-ross-saving-orwell

It is clear that Trump's election and the sequence of bizarre events that succeeded his swearing in, have alerted the public to the danger Trump poses to democratic freedoms and the danger that under an authoritarian personality like Trump's, the US, for all its vaunted talk as the bastion of democracy, could join the small but growing number of dictatorships around the world. Even if was written 60 plus years ago, few other texts speak so forcefully about such key subjects of our political culture as authority, surveillance, freedom of speech and thought, and the nature of power itself. And few other novels tap so directly into our anxieties about being watched, monitored and speaking our minds.

Here is a novel of ideas that is also a gripping thriller, as one individual seeks to resist the oppressive forces of his totalitarian society and escape not only with his life but arguably, more importantly, with his soul. Little wonder then that in a time of crisis, with politicians constantly talking about threats to the country from both within and from without to provide arguments for foreign wars and heightened security measure, *1984* became the book of the moment.

Why Orwell Wrote the Novel

Yet whilst we must understand the contemporary relevance of *1984*, we also need to appreciate that the novel also belongs to its particular time and is an expression of Orwell's response to the events which he witnessed and in which he participated. The rise of Fascism in Germany was one such event as was the fight to defeat Franco in Spain – a fight that Orwell joined and suffered a serious wound as a result. Here he was involved not only in the struggle against authoritarianism from the Right but also in seeking to defend democracy from the attempts of the Soviet communists to hijack the Republican cause. After the Spanish Civil War then, Orwell had few illusions about communism in action, for he had seen how propaganda and a biased press can manipulate people's attitudes and bend the truth. To put it simply, Orwell knew what he was writing about in *1984* and thus as long as totalitarian ways of thinking and governing continue to operate in our society, his novel will remain relevant. What matter is that we don't view it as a prophecy about a future society and pick holes in its predictions – as yet homes don't have telescreens that can keep tabs on our private lives – but as a warning of what can happen if we don't do enough to resist individuals or institutions that have little or no interest in the maintenance of democracy.

Key parallels between novel and contemporary times

In teaching *1984* to students it is important that they are enabled to recognize the different ways in which Orwell's vision of a totalitarian society bears similarities to certain potentially emergent tendencies in our own society.

To start with, we may note how the citizens of Oceania are encouraged to live in a permanent state of crisis. The constant news reports of foreign wars, the constant focus on the dangers of dissent to the stability of society and the constant emphasis on whipping up of a sense of hatred against enemies of the state can be paralleled by the efforts of recent politicians and media outlets to stoke a sense of anxiety, or even panic, in our own culture.

Selecting foreign countries for attack because of their links with terrorism, scapegoating migrants for the same reason and making the case for new security measures to protect people from the terrorist threat all help contribute to a sense that drastic measure to curb free speech and stifle opposition have a real and pressing justification. Totalitarianism thrives in times of crisis as Orwell well understood.

The Party also maintains a tight control of society by doing all it can to shape people's ideas of the world. Thus, there is a department of state in the Ministry of Truth – one that Winston Smith works for - devoted to the re-writing history in order that historical records reflect the Party's version of the past. In addition, with total control of the media and a continual outpouring of propaganda in the form of films, books, pamphlets, posters etc., there is virtually no space for alternative opinions. Western democracies pride themselves on a free press and television service but there is little doubt that there are ongoing pressures, whether from commercial or political interests, to construct a particular version of the world – a version that serves to promote one set of values and priorities over another.

Furthermore, with the attempts by the current US president to discredit news reporting and suggest that `facts` are fabrications made up by the president's enemies, the pressure on the media to stay silent or distort the truth has intensified. Compared to the world of *1984*, our's possesses considerably more freedom but to protect and strengthen it we need to be vigilant and with this Orwell's novel can certainly assist.

With telescreens, surveillance cameras, thought-police and citizen spies, the Party has enormous capacity to monitor people's lives – both their everyday activities and innermost thoughts. From the first pages of *1984*, when Winston has to find an unobserved corner of his room to start his diary, Orwell shows readers how difficult and dangerous it is for individuals to think their own thoughts and this theme runs through the novel as he seeks to continue his relationship with Julia. Care has always to be taken to avoid observation and thus arrest, until the moment comes when the Thought-Police invade the sanctuary he believed he had created over a junk shop.

Trump is engaged like Oceania's ruling party in *1984* with a war on truth. Ross notes that according to the Washington Post, Donald Trump made 492 false or misleading claims during his first 100 days in office. [11]Ross quotes Rebecca Gordon, a professor of philosophy at the University of San Francisco and expert on torture, notes that topics that do not fit in with the Trump agenda such as climate-change and the justice of the travel ban against Muslims, have been removed from federal websites. The present administration, Gordon argues, like Oceania's Ministry of Truth "seems intent on tossing recent history down the memory hole." The strategy is a deliberate one, according to Gordon a "grinding away at American memories" as a method of imposing the new president's narrative and will on the public – a method consistent with Orwell's belief, articulated in *1984*, that "Who controls the past," "controls the future: who controls the present controls the past."

We may not have tele-screens but we certainly have much of the apparatus of the secret state – an apparatus made far more sophisticated and powerful by technology. Computers and mobile phones certainly allow us to do many things Orwell and his fellow-citizens could only dream about but such devices, together with the techniques Orwell highlighted, allow the State to identify dissent almost before it has emerged. There may well be strong arguments for western governments to have increased surveillance powers – for example, to gather mobile phone data on a massive scale – as Edward Snowden revealed – but *1984* should alert us to the potential consequences. Big Brother may not be such a noticeable presence in our society as he was in Oceania but he is nevertheless alive and well.

---

[11] http://bostonreview.net/literature-culture/peter-ross-saving-orwell

Very near the beginning of *1984* Orwell depicts hate-week, which seems to be an opportunity for the Party to stir up the populace into a frenzy of hatred through the showing of film-footage of Oceania's enemies, both foreign and internal. Even Winston finds it impossible to join in the audience's emotional outbursts – although he may be dissembling. Through creating an intense and total hatred for the enemy enables those in power to divert people's energies and discontents on to an Other, whether this be the traitor Goldstein or East Asia.

More generally, both as presidential candidate and president, Trump has sought to appeal to latent feelings of xenophobia in American society – whether directed against Mexicans, migrants or foreigners. The slogan "America First"- a slogan first .. , is a slogan that makes its impact by excluding those who, for whatever reason, can be regarded as different – or at least different from the idea of America that Trump represents. And, if you are inside the tent, your allegiance is absolutely clear, as is your enemy. Thus, both Orwell and Trump understand the political value of hatred against the Other in pursuing and strengthening power.

Reading *1984* may allow students to understand how politicians make rhetorical use of their opponents to bolster their own popularity. Think, for example of the ways in which Candidate Trump attacked Hillary Clinton with an unprecedented level of personal vitriol in his speeches and the way in which he used his campaign rallies to stir up animosity against a whole range of individuals and institutions that he disliked. Little wonder them, that in the manufactured hysteria he and his collaborators created, violence was never far from the surface.

To arouse people's emotions, whether they be hate or love, requires language – something that Orwell was very much aware of. There are certainly examples in *1984* of political rhetoric used to shape attitudes but the novel's central insight relates to the idea of newspeak. If a fully-functioning democratic society thrives on communication between people and their representatives and between people, then curtailing the means by which this happens through eliminating certain words or simplifying the available vocabulary, is a powerful way to erode that democracy. Thus, straight-forward assertions replace conflicting and complex arguments about policy and the expression of possible subtlety or nuance. Furthermore, by engaging in doublethink, a formulation that allows an individual to hold contradictory thoughts in their head at the same time, citizens can, for example, believe that their country is both at war and at peace or that the threat of terrorism is increasing and diminishing.

Politicians have always sought to adapt their language to their audience, so as to communicate with potential voters more effectively but an examination of the speeches and twitter postings of candidate and President Trump reveals a politician who has taken this tendency to the extreme. With the use of a restricted vocabulary, repetition and a basic syntax, Trump's language conveys simplistic messages that reinforce the assumptions and prejudices of his audience. As to doublethink, one good example might be the government's declared policy towards China – for this country is both responsible for damaging the US's economic prosperity and is also a strong ally in the struggle against north Korea.

Orwell also recognized that a ruling elite could maintain its power by ensuring that the masses were not encouraged to engage in too much political thinking. As Winston notices as he wanders through London`s streets, the Proles are too busy enjoying themselves in the pubs to have any time to reflect on the reality of their situation. Fed a diet of pornography and popular music, the Party has effectively eliminated any threat to the status quo they might potentially have posed.

Of course, in spite of the fact that we too have a vibrant popular culture and multiple distractions, ordinary people in western democracies do take an interest in politics and do have the chance to vote in elections. Yet, with an ex reality tv star in the White House and with both himself and several members of his family closely connected to today's pervasive celebrity culture, we need to recognize how it serves politicians` interests for the mass of the people to be more occupied with the stuff of tabloid magazines than serious politics. If we are preoccupied with Beyonce, we are less likely to be preoccupied by the latest attempts to water-down climate change regulation.

Initial Activities

Pre-reading

- Watch the following YouTube videos to discuss how they differ

This 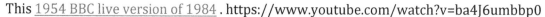1954 BBC live version of 1984 . https://www.youtube.com/watch?v=ba4J6umbbp0

" The production proved to be hugely controversial, with questions asked in Parliament and many viewer complaints over its supposed subversive nature and horrific content. In a 2000 poll of industry experts conducted by the British Film Institute to determine the 100 Greatest British Television Programmes of the 20th century, Nineteen Eighty-Four was ranked in seventy-third position.."

This 1956 film (https://www.youtube.com/watch?v=fCZBnUt6

Loosely based on the novel and is the first cinema rendition of the story, directed by Michael Anderson, and starring Edmond O'Brien. Also starring are Donald Pleasence, Jan Sterling, and Michael Redgrave. Pleasence also appeared in the 1954 television version of the film, playing the character of Syme, which in the film was amalgamated with that of Parsons. O'Brien, the antagonist, was renamed "O'Connor," possibly to avoid confusion with lead actor Edmond O'Brien.

This 1985 adaption of 1984 starred John Hurt and Richard Burton and was well received at the box office.

The following Youtube video is the best version available but has circling stars that probably have been useful so that the copyright holders do not take it down from the Internet.
https://www.youtube.com/watch?v=ztQ9wmjpiT0

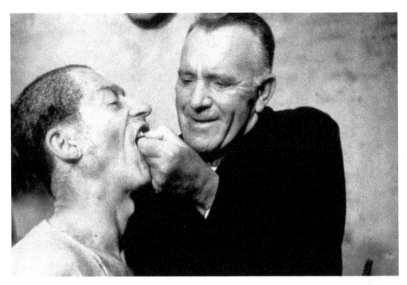

Richard Burton as O'Brien torturing John Hurt as Winston Smith

- After reading first few chapters, ask students to identify and discuss any similarities and/or differences they notice between the world of Oceania and their own society.

During Reading

- Ask students to re-write one chapter from the point of view of either Winston or Julia.

- Identify any moments in the novel where you thought that Winston`s resistance had a chance of success and discuss your reasons.

- Discuss why O'Brien refuses to execute Winston

After Reading

After reading the following statements about Winston's rebellion, rank them according to your level agreement

- Winston rebels for personal rather than political reasons
- Winston`s rebellion is a futile gesture – and he knows it
- Winston was naivity caused the failure of his rebellion

- How is power maintained in 1984?

- In what ways might Winston`s job be similar or dissimilar to the job of a journalist in today's society?

- Select a news report about a recent crime and re-write it to put the criminal(s) in a good light.

- Using the information about newspeak given in the novel, translate the following words into Newspeak:

- After reading the section on doublethink in the novel, write a short press release about an imaginary US President`s decision to ban the use of mobile phones in Washington DC in which you include some examples of doublethink.

- Suggest some reasons why the idea of a thought-police force may seem totally absurd and/or possible.

- Do you consider Winston's rebellion justified?

- Would Winston have been justified in using violence?

- How special is Winston or might many other people in his circumstances have chosen his path?

- What is the moment of his greatest defeat and why?

- Could Winston have used any other strategies to resist the system?

- Which passage in the novel do you find most terrifying and why?

Making Connections

- Discuss any similarities between the way power is maintained in Oceania and the way it is maintained in your society?

- Research and discuss the international developments of Orwell's time that influenced his writing of *1984*.

Talking Points
- Where does hope/resistance come from?
- Why is the idea of Big Brother such a fascinating/important one.
- What is the significance of the ending?
- Significance of the diary, images of paperweight, protecting arm etc

Concluding Words

We may have elections in our society but large groups of people still nevertheless feel, as witnessed by Brexit and the choice of outsider Donald Trump as President, that their voices don't count, either because of the voting system or the apparent collusion between representative parties. In other words, both for politicians in *1984*, and for politicians in many other countries, those outside the privileged elite can be regarded as of little real importance; a few may be given a small stake in the society to ensure its smooth functioning and the rest – the masses or the Proles - can be left to their own devices. Enabling student to recognize the similarities in how power is exercised, in spite of the differences, between Oceania and the US should provoke questions about what democracy really means and whether casting your vote every four or five years is a sufficient characteristic of a truly democratic society.

Chapter 3: Fahrenheit 451 and the Rise of Anti-Intellectualism

Trump's appeal has always been to the non-college educated working class voter. He has made no apologies for "loving" the "poorly educated voter." It is an uncomfortable truth that those who favor right wing parties, whether they be in France (National Front), the Netherlands (Freedom Party) and Germany (Alternative for Germany) or the UK (UKIP) are predominantly those who have not advanced beyond high school. You might begin your discussion on Bradbury's *Fahrenheit 451* after reading *1984* or after a particularly egregious Trumpian anti-intellectual act, such as taking down a government site on Climate change or cutting off medical or scientific research funds for an agency like NIH, with one of two questions:

1) Why do you think Trump cut funding etc for this program? (if there is a topical fit)

Or more conventionally,

2) What do the two books, *1984* and *Fahrenheit 451* have in common?

To answer the first question students might say that Trump is not that bright and does not want to spend money on stuff he does not understand or that he is opposed to climate change.

It might be worth a quick review of what Trump has done since he has been in office to wage war against science:

- In his first budget proposal he slashed EPA's funding by 31 percent, the Centers for Disease Control and Prevention's funding by 17 percent, the National Science Foundation's funding by 11 percent, and the Department of the Interior's funding by nearly 12 percent.

- Trump selected clearly unqualified candidates as heads of top scientific agencies. Instead of people like the Nobel Prize-winning physicist Steve Chu to head the Department of Energy, Trump appointed a TV Dancing with the Stars contestant who reportedly got Cs and Ds in physics and chemistry to oversee the nation's nuclear arsenal

- The Environmental Protection Agency removed a page that explained the causes and effects of climate change from its website

- The Interior Department's Twitter account was suspended for Tweeting out pictures comparing President Obama's 2009 Inauguration crowd to President Trump's much smaller turn-out .and created the unforgettable phrase "alternative facts"

As *Time* magazine has pointed out -

"Even before the election, Trump was a shameless peddler of scientific fictions — that climate change is a Chinese hoax; that vaccines cause autism. No sooner had he won than he conspicuously summoned Robert F. Kennedy, Jr., a leading anti-vaccine fabulist, to Trump Tower for a meeting. His transition team floated the possibility that Kennedy would be appointed to a position overseeing vaccine safety and effectiveness — though the team later denied that any such job had been offered, perhaps as a result of public blowback"

So why you can ask your group. Does his lack of intelligence explain it? He is after all a graduate from Wharton, a so-called ivy league school. Is there something deeper at work? Many have put forward the notion that Trump's undermining of science and truth is part of a "gas lighting" strategy that dictators are familiar with. The term "gaslighting" is taken from a 1944 by movie (Gaslight) starring Ingrid Bergman and Charles Boyer in which a husband (Jack Bellingham) terrorizes his wife Bella into questioning her sanity by blaming her for according to one source, "misplacing household items which he systematically hides. Doubting whether her perspective can be trusted, Bella clings to a single shred of evidence: the dimming of the gas lights that accompanies the late- night execution of Jack's trickery. The wavering flame is the one thing that holds her conviction in place as she wriggles free of her captor's control."

Trump's attacks on science go hand in hand with his attack on mainstream media as "fake news." The overall strategy is designed to make people question all authority, all facts and start trusting him and his delusionary view of the world. It is a classic strategy of dictators who want to keep in power - they seek to diminish the one weapon their critics have--the truth - by confusing people as to what the truth is and who might be telling the truth. As one psychologist stated, "The very state of confusion they are creating is a political weapon in and of itself. If you make people confused, they are vulnerable [...] You come in and undercut their trust in the established sources of information. It tells them to go ahead and hate this person who is delivering bad news. Then you begin to substitute your own news, your own version of reality...
"If Donald Trump can undercut America's trust in all media, he then starts to own them and can start to literally implant his own version of reality."

His targets are limited to the ones that he feels his base of supporters (largely high school educated voters) will not readily understand the significance of. For example, the climate change issue does not seem directly to affect their everyday lives as does much government supported research and development that Trump wants to cut. They are prime targets for conspiracy theories. Narratives are devised that seem to prove that experts cover up evidence and cannot be trusted. It is no coincidence that Trump loves a good conspiracy theory as they typically feature an over-reaching government that fixes evidence and silences enemies. The hero of the conspiracy theory is the teller of the conspiracy theory---the one who tells the truth and exposes the lies. This is the role that Trump has sought out for himself. They appeal particularly to the "low information voter"-- a synonym for Trump's core constituency--someone who is resentful of elites who, from their perspective, try to establish their superiority over them by using long words, and referencing history and books. As a self- confessed non-reader, Trump instinctively understands this person's mentality and can appeal to them.

The societies of both *1984* and *Fahrenheit 451* are run by people who are deeply afraid of history, truth, individual conscience and of course reading and books. Like Trump, if they cannot destroy alternative sources of information, they want to make people doubt or dismiss them or simply not have the capacity to think their way to understanding what kind of world their leaders have established. For example, the big battle in *1984* is to reduce the language down to some basic words that will eventually reduce the power to think dissident or rebellious thoughts. In Bradbury's novel, the idea is to destroy all books and eliminate reading to achieve roughly the same objective. One of the Newspeak engineers says, "[we're] cutting the language down to the bone . . ."In the end we shall make thoughtcrime literally impossible," explains the Newspeak engineer, "because there will be no words in which to express it"

You can ask the class at this point which strategy they view as most effective – destroying books or reducing language – in order to achieve complete control of the society? Which strategy in which countries was more practical in the society of 1950 and which is more practical today and in what countries? Given the nature of the discussion, it might be possible to revisit the Trump strategy. He is not yet a totalitarian leader but he does seem to be engaged in gaslighting and telling the big lies that only few people including Winston Smith have the mental fortitude to resist swallowing. Winston refers to the technique as 'Duckspeak'- to be effective, "you just say things frequently and people eventually understand and say it themselves" as it gets endlessly repeated through the words of the telescreens, newspapers and magazines. Some of the book's rare dark humor is provided by Winston's amazement that his co-workers swallow the lies that the media regularly spews out but the joke is on Winston, who has trouble in knowing whether Oceania is really at war with Eurasia or Eastasia. The difficulty is compounded by the fact that the Party keeps changing the historical records. Winston like everyone else begins to succumb to the belief that there is no independent reality that can be constructed like and so by the time of the novel's pessimistic conclusion he is willing to accept the Party's reality. For this form of brainwashing ('Duckspeak') to be effective, "you just say things frequently and people eventually understand and say it themselves" (Chilton 27). This brainwashing is done through the words of the telescreens, newspapers and magazines.

We can thank Fox News and Trump TV as the modern instruments of this form of duckspeak - let's call it Donald Duck speech.

We may be a long way yet from the reality depicted in *1984* but your class might agree that we have started down that awful road - a journey that Bradbury thought we might be on when he began writing *Fahrenheit 451* five years after *1984*. *Fahrenheit 451* arguably presents a more realistic description of the world we currently inhabit than Orwell's equally pessimistic glimpse into the future. While Orwell takes the reader into the inner workings of the Party apparatus and shows us how the brutal machinery of totalitarian government works to punish, if not "vaporise", individuals, who like Winston Smith, express the slightest hint of dissent, Bradbury indicates that only a minimal amount of coercion is necessary to keep the society stable and happy.

One telling example in terms of illustrating the two views is to look at the role television plays in each society. In *1984* the telescreen is as ubiquitous as its counterpart in *Fahrenheit 451* but it is primarily used as a propaganda tool--to provide the government documentaries and newscasts and to carry the ritualistic two minutes of hate, with a secondary function of surveillance. In *Fahrenheit 451* the telescreen is a wall-sized device in everyone's home that provides endless amounts of multichannel entertainment and infotainment. In *1984* information is limited and controlled by the government, in Fahrenheit 451 information and entertainment is so overwhelmingly plentiful it drowns out any capacity on the part of any individual to adequately respond. *Fahrenheit 451* presents a . It is a world not ruled by big brother as much by someone, like a Rupert Murdoch, who is all for giving people what they want. Thus, in a world of constant contests and quizzes, the winners are those who can remember words to "more popular songs or the names of state capitals or how much corn Iowa grew last Year." The schools are no better--full of classrooms where students "never ask questions" but are places where "answers are run at you" Where students are run "so ragged by the end of the day" that they "can't do anything but go to bed or head for a Fun Park to bully people around, break windowpanes in the Window Smasher place or wreck cars in the Car Wrecker. It is a world Trump would recognize since no one reads and where the word "intellectual" has become a swear word. It is a society without a memory --that exists in a continuous present filled with gossip about soap operas and films. Image and personality triumph over substance.

In a jaw dropping interview for the New Yorker, Tony Schwartz, Donald Trump's ghostwriter, for the best-selling, *Art of the Deal,* that propelled the New York property developer to national attention, acknowledged that the President has a "a stunning level of superficial knowledge and plain ignorance." [12]Among the astonishing insights derived after spending a year and a half in Trump's company is Schwartz's serious doubt as to whether "Trump has ever read a book straight through in his adult life." During the eighteen months that he observed Trump, Schwartz said, he never saw a book on Trump's desk, or elsewhere in his office, or in his apartment. Trump, Schwartz asserts has a painfully short attention span that has left him with "a stunning level of superficial knowledge and plain ignorance." It is the reason "why he so prefers TV as his first news source—information comes in easily digestible sound bites." Tony Schwartz now regrets his decision to ghost the book that accelerated Trump from being a show business billionaire to someone with some serious intellectual muscle. As Schwartz puts it in his characteristically blunt way, "I put lipstick on a pig," and feels "deep remorse."

There is, of course, a direct line that can be drawn from this anti-intellectualism that flows from Trump`s refusal to read or reflect to his bizarre statements, such as that climate change was "created by and for the Chinese in order to make U.S. manufacturing non-competitive."
He is proud of his own lack of learning, his own reliance on common sense without books or experts to confuse him. Trump has bragged about his own gut instincts as being in some ways superior to those of experts and how he reaches the "right decisions" "with very little knowledge other than the knowledge and 'common sense, (" because I have a lot of common sense") and business ability ("I have a lot of business ability."[13]) Trump's self-belief, even bravado leads him to assert that he knows "more about ISIS than the generals do, believe me." Trump wants us to see him as the consummate salesman, who believes knowledge or experience are secondary to gut instinct and that because his brand is so intimately tied to the idea that he is a super-star businessman, we have to, as he repeatedly says, "trust him" or as he likes to say more often "believe him." It was on such a basis that he asked us to believe in his accusation, without a scrap of evidence, that President Obama was born in Kenya and so was disqualified to serve as US President. He kept that fiction going well after the President produced his birth certificate.

---

[13] http://www.patheos.com/blogs/dispatches/2016/07/20/the-anti-intellectualism-of-donald-trump/

What has this to do with us --that we have a president who can back out of the Paris Climate change agreement and can believe he knows more than experts on any given issue?

How can you engage your class in a discussion on this matter? One way into the conversation is to engage them with the question-- how did one of the most educated nations in the history of the world, with more postgraduate degrees than anywhere on the planet, elect such an intellectually shallow not to say duplicitous man?

They may need some supplementary context. It is useful to remind them that history's trajectory has not been a smooth one from darkness to enlightenment. There there have been some eras when the elevator we thought we were all riding on suddenly stopped and without much warning headed back down to the basement. The lights did flicker and dim during these times but never quite went out.

Anti-Intellectualism in History

Montag and Winston Smith are intellectuals in the sense that they are constantly on the alert for the way their societies are prepared to pull the wool over their eyes and distort reality. These people are the veritable canaries in the coal mine-they sense danger way before ordinary human beings can and are prepared to go one step further than many intellectuals - they are prepared to suffer or even die for their convictions. It is important that in our class discussion we claim them as intellectuals and make clear that proto-fascist societies fear these people. It is the reason why once in power, dictators devote their time to denigrating them. Nazis were fond of such expressions degenerate intellectuals," "eggheads," "effete snobs," and referring to universities as "a nest of reds." Goering of course was famous for his alleged statement "When I hear talk of culture I reach for my gun"

Again, the question is why go after intellectuals. Before asking this question, it would be useful for us to view a slideshow that we have prepared on the special site devoted to this book on the long and sordid history of totalitarian rulers believing that they can destroy ideas and beliefs that threaten them by either burning the books that dissident authors produce or the authors themselves.

- The first historical example of such acts date back to the Chinese empire when somewhere between 59 and 210 B.C., the Chinese emperor, Shih Huang Ti, wanted to change the record book to show that history began with him and so he reportedly buried alive 460 Confucian scholars and in 212 B.C., he burned all the books in his kingdom, retaining only a single copy of each for the Royal Library and those were destroyed before his death.

- In 168 BC, Antiochus IV ordered that Jewish books in Jerusalem be "rent to pieces" and burned. The Emperor Constantine ordered the burning of works by those who disputed the Trinity. The Christian Emperor, Jovian, burned the library of Antioch in 364 AD, because it had been stocked largely by Emperor Julian who was non-Christian; and in 392 AD, the library at Alexandria was looted and burned by Christian mobs and the woman philosopher Hypatia murdered.

- Between 1497-98: Savonarola, destroyed books and paintings by some of Florence's greatest artists of Florence on the grounds that their "lines were wicked and impure".

- In 1525: Six thousand copies of William Tyndale's English translation of the New Testament were burned by the English Roman Catholic church, which determined that the Bible would be available only in Latin and therefore not available to the masses of people.

- In 1624: Martin Luther's German translation of the Bible was burnt in Germany by order of the Pope

Of course, the most notorious book burning episode was in 1933 when Nazi youth groups burned some 25,000 "degenerate" books at a large bonfire in Berlin. Included in the pyre were the works of John Dos Passos, Albert Einstein, Sigmund Freud, Ernest Hemingway, Helen Keller, Lenin, Jack London, Thomas Mann, Karl Marx, Erich Maria Remarque, Upton Sinclair, Stalin, and Leon Trotsky. These horrific events were repeated throughout Germany in the 1930s and 1940s, arguably the most educated nation in Europe. Freud would later joke "[w]hat progress we are making. In the Middle Ages they would have burned me. Now, they are content with burning my books." But Freud probably is fortunate he didn't stick around in Vienna after the Nazis annexed Austria to find out it that was true.

Getting back to the question as to why totalitarian leaders engage in denigrating intellectuals or their works--we might get a varied number of answers:

- Totalitarian societies are fragile in the sense that their one unifying idea is the omnipotent leader, who in his own person embodies the state, its cultural aspirations and its nationalistically defined history. To hold together they need scapegoats who, like Goldstein can be vilified as "enemies of the people." Intellectuals are easy targets--in the sense that they are often perceived as outsiders, elitist and different.

- Since comparatively few people actually read books while some despise the association books have with elitism and higher learning, burning them or throwing their authors in prison or killing them can have a unifying effect. Such radical acts are designed as powerful symbols to keep true believers in their camp and terrorize potential regime opponents. The two minutes of hate --a signature note of the *1984* society seems to serve all of these functions. In a similar way setting fire to people's homes as in *Fahrenheit 451* serves to release some primal emotions that signal that some unnamed enemy has been defeated and the community is stronger as a result.

- Some clues might be found in the strong American anti-intellectual movement that flourished in the middle of the 19th century, particularly under the sway of powerful evangelical preachers. It is the idea that there is only one good book, the Bible and the rest of the books published by man are distractions. Fire and brimstone preachers like the post-Civil war prelate Dwight L. Moody expressed the sentiment well when he stated "I have one rule about books.. I do not read any book, unless it will help me understand the book...I would rather have zeal without knowledge; and there is a good deal of knowledge without zeal." Billy Sunday, Moody's successor, ranted against the US trend towards forming a college educated nation, "thousands of college graduates are going as fast as they can straight to hell. If I had a million dollars i'd give $999,999 to the church and $1 to education...when the word of God says one thing and scholarship says another, scholarship can go to hell!" Such sentiments flourished particularly in the South, where the Book of Genesis battled it out with Darwin's theory of evolution in the famous Scopes Monkey trial.

The trial was the subject of an excellent film, *Inherit the Wind* (1960) starring Spencer Tracy as the famous lawyer Clarence Darrow; interestingly enough he loses the case.

Fahrenheit 451 helps us to address some of these themes in several ways.

1) The novel's central idea that when a society is so afraid of ideas that it resorts to book burning can be connected to Trump's core anti-intellectualism. The President's contempt for intellectuals, books, reading and complex ideas is reflected in several ways in Bradbury's novel but centrally is the idea that a society of non-readers is more stable and more compliant than one that it is not. Such a society is also more like the America Trump remembers from his youth--the more compliant society comfortable with top down authority as exercised by the military and in schools and universities and willing to fight in foreign wars even when the rationale for the war (Viet Nam) was murky at best.

2) As one of the characters in the book describes how the policy of book burning evolved we can hear troubling echoes of the Trump's campaign tactic to focus on the less educated among us for his appeal and his savaging of elites. "What is more easily explained and natural? With schools turning out more runners, jumpers, racers, tinkerers, grabbers, snatchers, fliers, and swimmers instead of examiners, critics, knowers, and imaginative creators, the word "intellectual, of course, became the swear word it deserved to be."

3) Trump also showed during the campaign how much he relished violence. He routinely egged on the crowd to commit violence against hecklers or dissenters and Trump's inner bully boy was often on display in other ways when he made fun of a disabled reporter or encouraged police to rough up their victims. In his novel, Bradbury has one of his characters express the view that the firemen are justified because they are simply acting out the schoolboy hatred of the nerd. The idea might have been taken from one of Trump's speeches. "Surely you remember the boy in your own school class who was exceptionally 'bright,' did most of the reciting and answering while the others sat like so many leaden idols, hating him. And wasn't it this bright boy you selected for beatings and tortures after hours? Of course, it was. We must all be alike. Not everyone is born free and equal, as the

> Constitution says, but everyone is made equal - which gets us right back to the Asimov quote--my ignorance is as good as your knowledge.

> 4) Firemen were the enforcers of the new ethic that everyone must be made to be equal in the sense that their individuality is crushed along with their imagination and voice. The firemen were "given the new job, as custodians of our peace of mind, the focus of our understandable and rightful dread of being inferior; official censors, judges, and executors. That's you, Montag, and that's me."

The US, with its fascination with celebrity, rich people, rock stars and ratings and with its belief in winners and losers is of course partly responsible for Trump. Trump could only occur in America. Only in the US can a billionaire can be taken seriously as the voice of an oppressed white working class "silent majority." The underlying assumption can be traced back to America's founding, when there was a basic agreement that democracy meant that everyone no matter his wealth or background was fundamentally equal and had a right to express their views no matter what. Over time, this view that everyone was entitled to his own belief has in this modern era of celebrity degenerated into a view that facts and expertise are not critical. It just matters whether the person sincerely expresses his or her views – an idea that encourages anti-intellectualism - a contempt for experts who would stand between an honestly held belief and its utterance. As the late Isaac Asimov, the prolific science fiction author, has written, "Anti-intellectualism has been a constant thread winding its way through our political and cultural life, nurtured by the false notion that democracy means that 'my ignorance is just as good as your knowledge.'"

Present Dangers

This well-spring of anti-intellectualism has always been available to politicians who have used it to justify everything from segregation to refusing to set any limits to selling guns or armor piercing bullets even to mentally disturbed people. What is new is that in 21st century US we have all kinds of ways to take the minor strains of intellectualism global. You might discuss with your students the way that the Internet allows for extremist groups to find each other and to spread their propaganda--everyone from ISIS to Neo Nazis are able to get their so -called message out, recruit followers and otherwise organize their way to mainstream attention.

Then we have billionaires, with all kinds of bizarre opinions, ready to fund foundations and obtain dubious historians and scientists to give a veneer of respectability to false ideas and dress fakery up as knowledge. As Bill Moyers memorably puts it, "Thanks to these overlapping and mutually reinforcing segments of the right-wing media-entertainment- "educational" complex, it is now possible for the true believer to sail on an ocean of political, historical, and scientific disinformation without ever sighting the dry land of empirical fact."

Fahrenheit 451 helps us to address some of these themes in several ways.

1) The novel's central idea that when a society is so afraid of ideas that it resorts to book burning can be connected to Trump's core anti-intellectualism. The President's contempt for intellectuals, books, reading and any complex ideas is reflected in several ways in the book but centrally in the idea that a society of non-readers is more stable and more compliant than one that it is not. It is also more like the America Trump remembers from his youth--the more compliant society comfortable with top down authority as exercised by the military and in schools and universities and willing to fight in foreign wars even when the rationale for the war (Viet Nam) was murky at best.

2) As one of the characters in the book describes how the policy of book burning evolved we can hear troubling echoes of the Trump's campaign to focus on the less educated among us for his appeal and his savaging of elites, "What is more easily explained and natural? With school turning out more runners, jumpers, racers, tinkerers, grabbers, snatchers, fliers, and swimmers instead of examiners, critics, knowers, and imaginative creators, the word "intellectual, of course, became the swear word it deserved to be."

3) Trump also showed during the campaign how much he relished violence. He routinely egged on the crowd do commit violence against hecklers or dissenters Trump's inner bully boy was often on display in other ways when he made fun of a disabled reporter or encouraged police to rough up their victims. In the novel, Bradbury has one of the characters who feels that the firemen are justified because they are simply acting out the schoolboy hatred of the nerd. The lines might have been taken from one of Trump's

speeches. "Surely you remember the boy in your own school class who was exceptionally 'bright,' did most of the reciting and answering while the others sat like so many leaden idols, hating him. And wasn't it this bright boy you selected for beatings and tortures after hours? Of course it was. We must all be alike. Not everyone born free and equal, as the Constitution says, but everyone made equal.' - which gets us right back to the Asimov quote--my ignorance is as good as your knowledge

4) Firemen were the enforcers of the new ethic that everyone must be made to be equal in the sense that their individuality is crushed along with their imagination and voice. The firemen were " given the new job, as custodians of our peace of mind, the focus of our understandable and rightful dread of being inferior; official censors, judges, and executors. That's you, Montag, and that's me." (Seems to repeat earlier section)

Chapter 4: The Hunger Games

The sales of *The Hunger Games* since its publication in 2008 have been phenomenal. There are over 17 million copies of the book in print and 19 million for the two sequels, *Catching Fire* (10 million) and *Mockingjay* (9 million). This is just in the US alone. Of course, the movie has become one of the most lucrative franchises of all time.

The first question to ask students is why? What do they think has contributed to the phenomenal success of the book and its sequels?

Could it be that the kind of disconnection between those in power and those who suffer under its thumb has grown wider every day? Could it be that the entertainment values that the ruling class depicted in the novel remind us of our own plutocrats with their outlandish lifestyles and love of cruel bloodthirsty sports such as fox chasing, big game hunting and the like, seem only a few degrees away from the decadent rulers of Panem?

The Surprising Source of Inspiration for Hunger Games

The next question that might be asked is does *The Hunger Games* anticipate Trump and if so in what ways? The clue to the Trump connection was provided by the author Suzanne Collins herself but would be useful to see how many of our students can guess it. One source of Collins' inspiration came from reality television programs. She says that like the Panem games, the reality shows are broadcast across the country and they are watched by millions. The eureka moment for Collins came to her when one night, feeling tired, she started channel-surfing and on one channel she saw people competing for some million dollar prize and then saw footage of the Iraq war. In a video you might have your class view she describes how the two images "fused together" in an "unsettling way." Of course, Trump made his name in reality TV. Before becoming the star on *The Apprentice*, he was basically known as a failed New York playboy and wannabee tycoon who had suffered numerous bankruptcies. Almost overnight he became rebranded as a competent businessman, who epitomized capitalistic success by uttering his trademark "you're fired" at anyone who he judged as less than adequate entrepreneurs.

The next question to ask our students is how did a reality show host become president--is it because TV recast his personality in such a way that he looked and sounded if not presidential at least like a level headed, no-nonsense businessman who could solve thorny problems? Is it because he was so good on television that it did not matter that he routinely stiffed contractors, took advantage of so many tax loopholes that he ended up paying zero taxes for a number of years? TV bestowed on Trump some magical powers that politicians would kill for - except he was not a politician. The rest of course is history.

Walls

Of course, the society of Panem, in spite of the alphabetical nod to America (think Pan-Am) seems a very different one to the USA. However, although there is no real equivalent to the Games and the heartless violence that surrounds them, Collins` fictional world, like the worlds of all good science-fiction novels, bears the imprint of our own, if in an exaggerated and distorted form.
Students can be asked to recall a few of the science-fiction novels they have read and note down some similarities and differences with *The Hunger Games*.

Thus, the poverty and hardship of District 12, based as it is on mining and rugged countryside, resembles that to be found in places like West Virginia and parts of Appalachia, where people work hard but still find themselves scrambling to make ends meet. District 12 is, of course, hemmed in by a heavily guarded fence. Students might be asked why this is. Is it because as the government states, it is designed to keep dangerous wild life at bay or is there another motive? It might be at this time we can raise the issue of the wall that Trump insists must be built on the Mexican border to keep the US from being overwhelmed by "rapists and criminals" coming through the southern border.

Students can be asked to examine some of President's Trump's statements about why a wall is necessary and consider to what extent travel bans and similar forms of restriction on people`s movement are also examples of trying to separate people into distinct tribes. By segregating people in this way and stigmatizing and persecuting them at the same time, the state can wield power over them and if needs be unite the country against them, seen as they are as plotting to take over or to undermine the nation in some way. The parallels to the plight of Jews, Gypsies and other non-

Aryans in 1930s` Germany can be drawn here, for then and there as well, the government moved to first identify them--in the case of the Jews it was through the wearing of the gold star - then round them up into carefully patrolled ghettos and then commit mass genocide.

Spectacle

The shadow of Hitler's Germany is not far away from Collins' imagined world of Panem. The Nazis knew how to create spectacle and through spectacles like the infamous Nuremberg rallies convey the awesome power of the state and its leaders as almost super-human forces ready to crush individual dissent.

As we read the description of the pre-Games parade of the Tributes, with its reference to giant screens, the theatrical lighting, the `pounding music` and the crowds `going nuts`, students, without too much teacher prompting, might be reminded of President Trump`s rallies, both before he was elected and since, in which there is a deliberate and largely successful attempt, to create events that are intended to speak to people's instincts. Teachers can remind students of President Trump`s rallies by showing video-clips of them and asking students to analyze the sources of their emotional impact or to write about one of them in the voice of a Trump supporter.

Architecture

Teachers can also make students aware of how the State's power is also on display in the architecture of the Capitol. When Katniss and Peeta first arrive by train they are awestruck by the `grandeur` of the `magnificence of the glistening buildings in a rainbow of hues that tower into the air`. Compared to their own home town in District 12, this is a place that visibly and openly asserts authority and status – an authority and status also declared in such symbols of power as the seal of the Capitol and its anthem. Hitler with the help of his architect Albert Speer wanted to redesign Berlin to resemble something like Ancient Rome with massively scaled buildings that in Hitler's own words would "only be comparable with ancient Egypt, Babylon or Rome. What is London, what is Paris by comparison!" According to one report, his new capital, Germania would have involved "the construction of two main boulevards, 120 meters (131 yards) wide and running cross-shaped through the city, lined with a number of gigantic buildings, halls, squares and triumphal arcs."

Students might be asked to design their own Capital and related symbols to demonstrate the power of the State. They could also design a capital city that embodied other values – eg democracy, freedom, community. This might be the moment when students could begin to ask themselves how a society's values are reflected in its art and architecture.

History as Propaganda

A further significant way in which President Snow`s regime secures its power is through creating and reinforcing a particular version of history – a version that suggests the debt of gratitude the populace owes to its leader. If President Trump presents himself as the saviour of the white working and middle class, rescuing them from a willfully neglectful establishment, the messages issued by Snow's regime, in the form of District 12 mayor's speech at the start of the Reaping, for example, or in the school lectures children across the country receive, tells the history of Panem as a story of triumph over natural disasters, war and finally rebellion - a triumph only enabled because of the wisdom, benevolence and strength of the nation's rulers. Students can be asked to research some historical myths and, for one or two, identify the source of their appeal. One myth, in particular, was one that Hitler spun that around the idea that Germany had been somehow "stabbed in the back" – a myth that helped propel him to power.

Teachers will also want to probably emphasize that the Government of Panem's grip on power is also maintained by an extensive system of surveillance and censorship. From the opening moments of the novel, we are made aware that the country's citizens are constantly alert to the possibility that they are being watched. Thus, Katniss has trained herself not to speak out about the things that are troubling her for fear of the consequences - `So I learned to hold my tongue and to turn my features into an indifferent mask so that no one could ever read my thoughts` And through the remainder of the narrative, whether at the Reaping or before and during the Games, she is constantly aware of cameras watching and listening to what she says and does in an effort to monitor and shape what the public outside are able to hear and see. `I wonder`, she thinks at one point, `if the Gamemakers are blocking out our conversation because even though our conversation seems harmless, they don't want people in different districts to know about one another`.

Students can be asked to research different kinds of surveillance operating in the place where they live and discuss their purpose and value. Teachers might organize a debate on the issue. Students may identify and consider examples of how the Trump administration has been both the victim of advanced forms of surveillance and the perpetrator of such surveillance. If everyone is watched, then life becomes a spectacle – in other words people become performers, more conscious of how they are viewed than who they are. This is most evident in the arena, which becomes a frightening metaphor for a society in which the distinctions between reality and fantasy have become so blurred that the latter has replaced the former. Katniss is forced to become a TV celebrity, needing to shape her persona in order to please the audience – ordinary people and sponsors - watching their screens.

Teachers can ask students to consider the implications of historical narrative becoming a form of propaganda, in which factual truth is suppressed and then forgotten, in order to establish a national myth that will secure subjects' loyalty to the State. Other kinds of narrative are also used to shape people's understanding of reality. Effie Trinket, a kind of chaperone and guard to District 12's tributes, for example, talks of the way she has crafted the stories of her two tributes to emphasize their sacrifice and struggle and heighten their appeal. Students should thus gain an understanding that power is not just expressed in the police-force and armies but is embedded in the wider culture and thus in the thought-processes and mind-sets of the populace.

Students can be asked to read some campaign and similar political material to see if they can identify and analyze for effect one or two stories – eg stories to do with heroic individuals, triumphs over disaster, patriotism etc. Futhermore, they could find examples in the novel of moments in which Katniss is required to become extremely conscious of the image she is projecting and to discuss what Collins might be trying to say about the role of celebrity and image in modern American culture. Thus, she is styled by Cinna to achieve a certain look and coached by Haymitch for her tv interview so she can make the right impression. When Peeta wants her to hold hands with him, she complies, recognizing this is likely to win her popularity and increase her chances of survival. In Collins' novel then, the power of the State is reinforced by a culture in which media image and spin are paramount. As Haymitch says, `It's all a big show. It`s all how you're perceived`.

Resistance

If *The Hunger Games* explores the different ways - both direct and indirect - in which the State exercises control over its populace, teachers are likely to want their students to be aware of the novel's political interest in the alternative strategies that can be used to resist this control. From early on, we are conscious of the fact that Katniss has become adept at maintaining a private self into which the authorities cannot penetrate. Even turning her `features into an indifferent mask` and making only polite small talk in the public market` are methods to fend off the Capitol's intrusive power. Students can be asked to identify and share any occasions they have been wary of saying something in private for fear they might be overheard by someone in authority.

Psychologically small gestures of resistance matter, firstly for the individual concerned and secondly for demonstrating to others that they are not compelled to accept everything dictated by authority with total passivity. When Gale, for example, mimics Effie Trinket's Capitol accent, the humor of the moment, as Katniss acknowledges, is an `alternative` to the customary fear in which the citizens of District 12 live. Similarly, later, Haymitch's antics, which border on the anarchic, also serve to subvert the meticulous organizational planning of the Games. He may be an insider in his role as mentor to the two new tributes but in his drunken unpredictability, like Shakespeare's Fool, he is the outsider who cannot be completely controlled.

Students can be asked to identify and discuss anyone in their circle and in the wider society who might be considered as a challenge to the status quo or authority in some way. Human kindness, whether on a small-scale, as when Peeta throws the starving Katniss some bread, or on a larger scale, as when the latter character substitutes herself for her younger sister as a Tribute to fight in the Games, can also be viewed as a form of resistance, for acts of compassion or generosity assert an oppositional set of values in face of the dominant ideology of individual competitiveness – an ideology which the Games perfectly embody. Students might be asked to debate the issue of whether charity can have a political dimension and whether this is particularly true in the USA today.

As the narrative of *The Hunger Games* develops and the stakes for the two main characters increase, students can be alerted to the way questions about resistance - whether and how best to being the most pressing - become ever more urgent. Peeta, for example, despite recognizing the need to retain a strong sense of his own identity in the midst of what's going on all around him – Ì want to show the Capitol they don't own me`-, also recognizes that he will only have a chance of survival and perhaps of resisting the power of the State, if he adopts a strategic approach. As Katniss notes, he makes sure that in conversation he qualifies what could be interpreted as a rebellious statement- ¬I'd leave here` with praise `...but the food's prime`. Students can be asked to write a short drama script in which a character shows their resistance to a person in authority questioning them indirectly. The scripts can then be performed and discussed.

Katniss undertakes a more direct form of resistance when she collects some wild flowers to decorate the murdered body of her friend, Rue, who has been killed in the Games. Her action is more symbolic than anything else but in light of the fact that it asserts Katniss`s humanity to the whole viewing audience of Panem, it possesses considerable potential power. For those watching, the simple gesture of love and friendship is a reminder that it is possible to live in a different, more humane, way even when under the rule of a totalitarian State.

Less symbolic and more practical is Katniss's final act of rebellion when she pretends to act out a double-suicide with Peeta, in order to force the Capitol to allow two victors of the Games rather than the normal one. Faced with the strength implied by her apparent willingness to accept death, the State concedes, demonstrating that citizens with sufficient determination, strength of will and cunning to resist, can defeat its power.

Of course, President Snow is not over-thrown and his regime continues but it continues weakened and vulnerable to further threats to its authority. Students can be asked to make a list of some forms of resistance that could be used against one or two of the current administration's policies. They should share and rank their suggestions in order of perceived effectiveness. One type of resistance might be noted that the movie of the book was directly responsible for occurred recently. A gesture (a raised up hand with three middle fingers pressed together) used in *The Hunger Games* trilogy to express unity with people striving to survive, was used in 2014 by anti-government protesters in Thailand, and according to one report at least seven were arrested for it. Students can be asked to research examples of political resistance in the past and/or across the world today. Presentations are then prepared, delivered and discussed.

In conclusion, teaching *The Hunger Games* may feel like an unusual experience for both teachers and students who are more used to encountering texts from the canon in the classroom. However, it may also be a rewarding one, offering as it does several opportunities to engage with a number of current topical issues, several of which are more pressing and critical since the election of President Trump.

Whole-Novel Activities

There are many interesting and creative ways to follow up a reading of *The Hunger Games* :

1. Organize a debate as to whether TV reality shows can be viewed as just harmless entertainment or they might have negative effects.
2. In groups select three passages from the novel depict the operation of power in one form or another. After discussing these ask groups to assess to what extent are those forms of power present or not present in current societies either in the US or around the globe and how might they be resisted.
3. After discussing the ending of the novel, work out and write an alternative version that offers readers a different perspective on Katniss and Peeta's situation after the Games have been completed.
4. Imagine and write the letter/email Katniss sends home after the Games are finished, in which she expresses how her views about Panem and the Capitol have changed.
5. Note down some of the reasons a School Board might use to stop teachers using the book in the classroom and the arguments a teacher might use to defend its use.
6. Devise a board or computer games based on the novel.
7. Exchange your thoughts about the novel with students in other schools, both in the US and abroad.
8. Identify and compose five questions you would like to ask Suzanne Collins about her novel.

Chapter Five: The Bluest Eye: Resisting Trump's Racist Appeals

In a recent *New Yorker* column, Nobel Peace Award winner Toni Morrison asked to grapple with the question of how and why Trump, wrote, [14]

"On Election Day, ..both the poorly educated and the well-educated—embraced the shame and fear sowed by Donald Trump. The candidate whose company has been sued by the Justice Department for not renting apartments to black people. The candidate who questioned whether Barack Obama was born in the United States, and who seemed to condone the beating of a Black Lives Matter protester at a campaign rally. The candidate who kept black workers off the floors of his casinos. The candidate who is beloved by David Duke and endorsed by the Ku Klux Klan."

Morrison suggests powerfully that the reason for whites -young and old, rich and poor, - "eagerly " voting for this man had to do with a specific kind of American racial insecurity. "Unlike, any nation in Europe, the United States holds whiteness as the unifying force. Here, for many people, the definition of "Americanness" is color."

---

[14] https://www.newyorker.com/magazine/2016/11/21/aftermath-sixteen-writers-on-trumps-america#morrison

Published in 1970 Toni Morrison's first novel, *The Bluest Eye*, uncovers the myth that underlies all racism, that one color--white - is inherently superior--purer than that of other colors. The theme of the destructive ramifications of this basic myth on people's lives as both non-whites internalize the self- hatred and whites internalize their own sense of white privilege, is one that she explores in all of her novels Although a hard-hitting and emotionally powerful book that some teachers may have reservations about using as a classroom text, it is a must-read in the age of Trump for several reasons. First it shows us how complex human emotions are. In contrast to the simplified Presidential tweets, often which serve to promote his simplistic view of a world filled with heroes and villains (heroes being supporters and enemies who will not cow tail to his views), Morrison offers alternative perspectives on events and refuses the easy pleasures of a straightforward linear narrative.

Second, the novel helps students to understand how certain people's identity in a racist society is reduced, or even made invisible. Two passages, depending on the age and maturity of your students, might be discussed in this light-- the superbly written episode in which Pecola feels her invisibility when buying sweets from a white shopkeeper or in the disturbing scene in which a group of white men watch a young black couple have sex. However, Morrison seems to be less interested in the prejudices and abuses of individuals – terrible as these often are – as in the more systematic ways in which racial hierarchies are created and reinforced in American society through such media institutions as advertising and cinema.

Throughout the novel, Morrison shows, whether it be in the form of Pauline Breedlove's helpless fascination with Hollywood film-stars or, most tragically, in her daughter's belief that only the blue eyes of white people can offer her the beauty she craves, how many Afro-Americans are subjected to the racialised myths and lies transmitted through popular culture. Having lost a sense of their own southern community by moving north to better themselves, they are vulnerable to a competitive and racist white society that perpetuates itself, at least in part, through the stories it tells itself and others.

Preliminary Activities

There are many ways we can start warming students up to some of the novel's themes:

We can begin with a general activity designed to sensitize the students to race, particularly as depicted before and after the civil rights era. Ask students to research magazines of the 1940s and 1950s on the web and collect example of different kinds of racial stereotyping.

Another activity would be to have students review a series of Trump racist words and actions since the 1970s in a list compiled by Vox[15]

1973: The US Department of Justice — under the Nixon administration, out of all administrations — sued the Trump Management Corporation for violating the Fair Housing Act. Federal officials found evidence, amongst other accusations, that Trump had refused to rent to black tenants and lied to black applicants about whether apartments were available. Trump said the federal government was trying to get him to rent to welfare recipients. In the aftermath, he signed an agreement in 1975, agreeing not to discriminate to renters of color without admitting to discriminating before.

1980s: Kip Brown, a former employee at Trump's Castle, accused another of Trump's businesses of discrimination. "When Donald and Ivana came to the casino, the bosses would order all the black people off the floor," Brown said. "It was the eighties, I was a teenager, but I remember it: They put us all in the back."

1988: In a commencement speech at Lehigh University, Trump spent much of his speech accusing countries like Japan of "stripping the United States of economic dignity." This matches much of his current rhetoric on China.

1989: In a controversial case that's been characterized as a modern-day lynching, four black teenagers and one Latino teenager — the "Central Park Five" — were accused of attacking and raping a jogger in New York City. Trump immediately took charge in the case, running an ad in local papers demanding, "BRING BACK THE DEATH PENALTY. BRING BACK OUR POLICE!" The teens' convictions were later vacated after they spent seven to 13 years in prison, and the city paid $41

---

[15] Donald Trump's long history of racism, from the 1970s to 2017 https://www.vox.com/2016/7/25/12270880/donald-trump-racism-history, August 17, 2017

million in a settlement to the teens. But Trump in October said he still believes they're guilty, despite the DNA evidence to the contrary.

1991: A book by John O'Donnell, former president of Trump Plaza Hotel and Casino in Atlantic City, quoted Trump's criticism of a black accountant: "Black guys counting my money! I hate it. The only kind of people I want counting my money are short guys that wear yarmulkes every day. … I think that the guy is lazy. And it's probably not his fault, because laziness is a trait in blacks. It really is, I believe that. It's not anything they can control." Trump at first denied the remarks, but later said in a 1997 Playboy interview that "the stuff O'Donnell wrote about me is probably true."

1992: The Trump Plaza Hotel and Casino had to pay a $200,000 fine because it transferred black and women dealers off tables to accommodate a big-time gambler's prejudices.

2000: In opposition to a casino proposed by the St. Regis Mohawk tribe, which he saw as a financial threat to his casinos in Atlantic City, Trump secretly ran a series of ads suggesting the tribe had a "record of criminal activity [that] is well documented."

2004: In season two of *The Apprentice*, Trump fired Kevin Allen, a black contestant, for being overeducated. "You're an unbelievably talented guy in terms of education, and you haven't done anything," Trump said on the show. "At some point you have to say, 'That's enough.'"

2005: Trump publicly pitched what was essentially *The Apprentice:* White People vs. Black People. He said he "wasn't particularly happy" with the most recent season of his show, so he was considering "an idea that is fairly controversial — creating a team of successful African Americans versus a team of successful whites. Whether people like that idea or not, it is somewhat reflective of our very vicious world."

2010: Just a few years ago, there was a huge national controversy over the "Ground Zero Mosque" — a proposal to build a Muslim community center in Lower Manhattan, near the site of the 9/11 attacks. Trump opposed the project, calling it "insensitive," and offered to buy out one of the investors in the project. On *The Late Show With David Letterman*, Trump argued, referring to Muslims, "Well, somebody's blowing us up. Somebody's blowing up buildings, and somebody's doing lots of bad stuff."

2011: Trump played a big role in pushing false rumors that Obama — the country's first black president — was not born in the US. He even sent investigators to Hawaii to look into Obama's birth certificate. Obama later released his birth certificate, calling Trump a "carnival barker."

2011: While Trump suggested that Obama wasn't born in the US, he also argued that maybe Obama wasn't a good enough student to have gotten into Columbia or Harvard Law School, and demanded Obama release his university transcripts. Trump claimed, "I heard he was a terrible student. Terrible. How does a bad student go to Columbia and then to Harvard?"

Ask students to list which ones of the statements are the most objectionable and why. Which ones resonate with *The Bluest Eye* and the sense that some feature like color or racial ethnic identity that the individual does not fully control means that the person is entitled to less dignity and respect than another person?

Reviewing the Novel

There are several ways in which teachers can approach the novel in the classroom but probably focusing on the author's presentation of each of the main character's response to the world they inhabit - the most straight-forward approach - will be the best.

Teachers might wish to begin with the characterisation of Claudia MacTeer, whose voice - first as an adult looking back and then as a child – we hear from early on as she relates her childhood experiences of home in a strict but loving family and at school. From the start, the theme of blame is hinted at in Claudia's realization that it was her and her sister's belief that it was either Pecola's illegitimate baby which prevented the marigolds in their yard from growing or that it was the fact that she had planted the seeds too far down, was mistaken.

- Ask students to identify occasions when they have wrongly attributed blame - to themselves or others - as a way of initiating a discussion of the temptations of scapegoating etc.

- Students could be asked to explore how racism is internalized through examining passages in which Morrison explores Claudia's hostile feeling towards her peers, for example, in the following - "We stare at her ... wanting to poke the arrogance out of her eyes and smash the pride of ownership that curls her chewing mouth." The hostility suggested here is underlined and developed in the depiction of Claudia's hatred of the image of Shirley Temple (a child film star of the 1940s) and the blonde dolls she receives as gifts with the expectation that they will be gratefully received: "From the clucking sounds of adults I knew that the doll represented what they thought was my fondest wish. I was bemused by the thing itself, and the way it looked. What was I supposed to do with it? Pretend I was its mother?" Looking back at her childhood feelings, the adult narrator is appalled: "I destroyed white baby dolls. But the dismembering of dolls was not the true horror. The truly horrifying thing as the transference of the same impulses to little white girls. The indifference with which I could axed them was shaken only by my desire to do so."

  Yet, although Claudia is horrified by how she feels and what she does, Morrison wants her readers to recognize what lies behind her character's behavior – a desire to understand the secrets of perceived white superiority: "What made people look at them and say ``Awwww`` but not for me?" To what extent you may want to ask your students do her attitudes and actions enable her to maintain a strong sense of identity at least temporarily. To what extent is this resistance preferable, to the `fraudulent love` and `delight in cleanliness` that the character acquires later - `an adjustment without improvement`?

- Ask students` to discuss their views of Claudia in these early pages of the novel. Might we expect white and black readers to react differently? What might enable white readers to value Claudia`s feelings and behavior? An opportunity to introduce the concepts of resistance and empathy. Morrison' presentation of Claudia's response to the racially and class divided society in which she grows up is developed further and made more complex through the rest of *The Bluest Eye*. Teachers will, probably, for example, wish students to consider her response to wealthy Maureen Peel, `a high-yellow dream-child`, who enchants the `entire school`. Looking for flaws but also helplessly attracted, Claudia and her sister dislike her at the same time as they are `fascinated` by her. They can`t help acknowledge she is `cute` but if this was the case `then we were not`. And what did that mean? We were lesser. Nicer, brighter, but still lesser. Dolls we could destroy, but we could not destroy the honey voices of parents and aunts, the obedience in the eyes of our peers, the slippery light in the eyes of the teachers when they encountered the Maureen Peals of the world. What was the secret? What did we lack? Here then, the author shows us how we start to form our identity, outlook on the world and arguably our politics too, through our personal relationships - relationships inescapably rooted in the racial and class divisions of our society. Thus, even as Maureen becomes the object of hatred and envy, the narrator knows that she isn't the real issue: And all the time we knew that Maureen peal was not the Enemy and not worthy of such intense hatred. The Thing to fear was the Thing that made her beautiful, and not us.

- By the end of *The Bluest Eye* Claudia's understanding of her society and the role that scapegoating has played, has significantly increased. Teachers will probably want to focus on this concept of scapegoating and direct their students' attention to the forcefully written passage in which the adult narrator states her view of the relationship between victim, in this case Pecola, and oppressor: ``All of us – all who knew her – felt so wholesome after we cleaned ourselves on her. We were so beautiful when we stood astride her ugliness. Her simplicity decorated us, her guilt sanctified us, her pain made us glow with health… we honed our egos on her, padded our characters with her frailty, and yawned in the fantasy of our strength''.

Here then, Morrison, through her main protagonist, expresses the crucial political and social insight that the powerful only achieve and sustain their power though creating an Other, who they can denigrate and de-humanize. Teachers may want to explore the idea of the Other and othering with their students before emphasizing that the powerful in this context are not necessarily those with status and wealth but the community itself, which, in its exposure of the vulnerable to different forms of racism and in its refusal to protect those damaged by such exposure, fails some of its members. Instead of real compassion then, the relatively privileged chose to substitute false values – "We substituted good grammar for intellect; we switched habits to simulate maturity; we rearranged lies and called it truth". Of course, Claudia and Morrison's anger is directed against a northern black community of an earlier generation but the ethical accusation reaches beyond a specific place or time to our own historical moment – a moment when our whole society seems set on creating others to despise and replacing empathy with prejudice.

- Ask students to discuss whether they think the adult Claudia is being too judgmental in her criticisms at the end of the novel. They can also be invited to come up with examples of their own failures to show empathy and failures that feature in recent news reports. A further discussion could be held regarding how important empathy is for a leader.

If Claudia's family provide a relatively stable and loving home for her and her sister, the same cannot be said for the other main family presented in the novel – the Breedloves. Whilst, Morrison offers an almost idyllic portrait of the parents' courtship and early married life, it soon becomes apparent, through her depiction of the individual stories of the couple, that their happiness has weak foundations because of the racially marked social worlds in which each has grown up. Cholly has suffered the trauma of losing the only person who cared for him at a young age and then being exposed to the humiliation of having his first sexual encounter observed and orchestrated by a group of white racists.

- Damaged as husband and parent, teachers will probably need to help students gain a sense of what the author is trying to convey through the characterisation. In what ways, for example, can he be said to be free, as articulated in the passage that begins 'The pieces of Cholly's life could become coherent only in the head of a musician ...' (p159) and how should we respond to his rape of his own daughter, Pecola? Here Morrison seems to be challenging us, as readers, to confront the worst aspects of human nature to test our own capacity for empathy. In the relevant section of the novel, we are invited to view what is happening through the rapist's viewpoint rather than that of the victim. There is violence and there is horror and there are terrible consequences to the act but also author writes of Cholly's 'tenderness' and 'protectiveness' - words that seem designed to shock and appall in this context.

- Ask students about their attitude to Morrison's depiction of the rape and their opinion concerning what Morrison was trying to achieve in the scene. Is it possible to empathize with someone who commits a terrible crime if we know they are psychologically damaged?

- The portrait of Pauline Breedlove also dramatizes, in a different way, how growing up and living in a racially divided society can erode people's sense of identity and humanity. How, for example, is it possible for her to seem to prefer the white child she is paid to look after to her own child?

- After reading the relevant scene, ask students to suggest possible explanations for Pauleen's behavior. Students might suggest that the character's action can be accounted for by her upbringing or by the various influences she is subjected to. Morrison certainly wants her readers to appreciate that it needs to be understood as the culmination of previous experiences rather than as straight-forward moral failing. There is, for example, the scene Pauleen recalls of delivering her baby in which the doctor refers to her as a `horse`, which seems to signify, in a dramatic way, how white professionals have permission to dehumanize black people.

However, even more telling and damaging is the influence of films, particularly romantic ones, on the character's identity and perceptions – an influence that distorts and substitutes fantasy for reality:

Along with the idea of romantic love, she was introduced to another – physical beauty -probably , according to Morrison, the most destructive idea in the history of human thought. Both originated in envy, thrived in insecurity, and ended in disillusion.

- Ask students to discuss the relevant passage and consider whether cinema and television can have such a significant impact on people as Morrison implies. Can film also be a force for social good? To cope with the disjunction between the reality of her life - a reality that includes domestic violence, the indifference of neighbours and the simple struggle to survive economically - Pauleen neglects her own home and family and turns to religion and respectability: "She became what is known as an ideal servant, for such a role filled practically all her needs…Here she found beauty, order, cleanliness, and praise". In the characterisation of Pauleen then, Morrison offers readers another type of response to a racially and socially divided America. If Claudia grows through anger to a kind of understanding and Cholly expresses his reactions to the dehumanizing circumstances of his life through violence, she takes on the role and values assigned to her by white culture, losing her own selfhood in the process.

The most extreme version of the latter kind of response is to be found in the character of Geraldine, whose embrace of respectable conformity results in her extreme reaction to the presence of Pecola in her home, brought there by her son: "She looked at Pecola. She saw the dirty torn dress, the plaits sticking out on her head, the hair matted where the plaits had come undone, the muddy shoes .." The girl then comes to represent all poor black people who disgust her: "Like flies they hovered; like flies they settled. And this one had settled in her house...."Get out," she said, her voice quiet. "You nasty little black bitch. Get out of my house."

Teachers will probably want their students to reflect on the sources of this disgust, as expressed in the relevant passage and introduce them to the possibility that behind the feeling lies a fear of being too close to them.

- Ask students to identify and discuss some of the various ways it is possible to respond to an oppressive situation. Can resistance, or even violent resistance, ever be justified?

Geraldine`s victim, Pecola, on who she projects her unconscious fear and conscious hatred, is arguably the central character in *The Bluest Eye*. Introduced early on indirectly as the guest in the McTeer`s home after her on home is burnt down by her father, Morrison's portrayal is both astute and heart-wrenching. Growing up with a sense of her own ugliness - `Please God... make me disappear`, - she sees her salvation, her way to achieving a sense of self-worth, through acquiring blue eyes. Unlike Claudia, she enjoys the Shirley Temple image on the cup and like Pauleen she comes to internalize white ideas of beauty.

Just once, after she buys some sweets from a local shop, do we gain a glimpse of a possible alternative response to the white dominated society in which she lives. Teachers will probably want students to examine the powerfully written scene in which Pecola buys some sweets – sweets with the image of a blond blue-eyed girl stamped on them. Sensing shop-keeper, Mr Yacobowski`s inability to see her as a person - `He does not see her, because for him there is nothing to see`- she becomes angry: "Anger is better. There is a sense of being in anger. A reality and presence. An awareness of worth. It is a lovely surging.` However, the anger doesn't last and from now on, shame is her main emotion – at her appearance but more significantly at who she is.

- After reading the scene, teachers might ask students to recall and share any episodes they have witnessed or in which they have participated, in which race has been a significant influence. Is anger always the best reaction to incidents of discrimination or prejudice? Pecola's fate, first at the hands of Geraldine and then at the hands of her father – the latter event leading to her pregnancy and the death of her baby - makes her mad. Believing, after her meeting with the paedophile, Soaphead Church, that she has been granted the blue-eyes she has passionately craved for so long, she loses touch with reality. Teachers may want their students to act out the interior dialogue that opens the final chapter of the novel before undertaking the following activity:

- Ask students for their interpretations of the dialogue and whether they believe Pecola's fate might have been avoided.

Given the emphasis in *The Bluest Eye* on the importance of empathy, it is worth noting that Soaphead, in spite of his sexual interest in children and in spite of his cruel deception of Pecola, is allowed to defend himself in his letter to God and is given some of the most resonant words in the novel: "You have to understand that, Lord. You said, "Suffer little children to come unto me, and harm them not." Did you forget? Did you forget about the children? Yes. You forgot". No-one – neither rapist or child-molester, Morrison seems to be saying can or should be excluded from the human community. At a time of walls and bans, the message is especially significant.

Partially framed at the start with an extract from a reading primer that features `perfect`, idealised white characters – a text that becomes increasingly disjointed as the novel proceeds – *The Bluest Eye* foregrounds the ways in which black people are psychologically damaged by the culture produced by a racially divided society. Officially, they may have equal rights but unofficially there is a sustained attempt to make them feel marginal and inferior.

Morrison wrote *The Bluest Eye* because `there were no books about me..` and certainly, there is little doubt that in spite of its refusal to romanticize black life and community, it is a novel that seeks to make sense of black experience and the social and political factors that underlie it. However, it is also a text that speaks beyond this topic and beyond America to a wider world – so in 2006, sixty-one years after the death of Hitler, it was selected as the annual Viennese One Town, One Book novel.

Trump`s America is a very different country from Nazi Germany and from the country about which Morrison is writing but as Fascist and racist attitudes of one kind or another are allowed to flourish and are normalized, so we need students to think carefully about how the ground that enables such attitudes to develop is nourished by the culture which surrounds us.

Whole Novel Teaching Activities

- Choose one episode from the novel that you consider the most important and explain the reasons for your choice
- Write an alternative ending for the novel
- Rewrite one scene from an alternative point of view, with an accompanying commentary explaining the difference the change makes
- Research those aspects of the 1960s context that are relevant to the novel
- Write a letter to Toni Morrison in which you make the case that the 1960s` slogan that `racial self-loathing` is, or is not, a major problem in today's society.
- Research the Clark doll test and explain its relevance to the novel.

Chapter 6 : Trump and Shakespeare

It is an understatement to say that Shakespeare was unusually perceptive about power--how it is acquired and at what cost and how it is given away? The bard understands rulers to be not exceptional human beings but tragic in that they typically have a set of what might be termed mental blind spots and obsessions that destroy them from within.

Enter Trump --a man singularly lacking in self-awareness, ready, like all the major Shakespearean characters, for action and for self- glorification but headed we all think for a fall. What could be a better way to start analyzing any of the great Shakespeare plays for clues to that odd personality he has--narcissism, bravado, ruthlessness etc etc. But we don't get very far when we compare Trump to any particular Shakespeare hero --that is because he lacks a certain amount of seriousness. He is more a buffoon than a real person--capable of experiencing shame, humility or embarrassment for his behavior. He is not self-aware enough to draw us into any kind of complex inner life because there seems no inner core there--just a bundle of self- presentations and survival skills. We might have better luck with members of his family--Ivanka and Jared seem straight out of King Lear (more about that later). They provide the mad king with the admiration and loyalty he so craves but behind his back are always calculating how far do they have to go to please the old man. When is the nut going to crack and when he does, how do they ensure that both their fortunes and reputations are secure?

Discussing Shakespeare and Trump together can have many educational benefits in that it can help students see the interaction of politics, history, morality and character in ways that are difficult to grasp using the standard textbook that describes one event after another as if they were all part of some predetermined grand narrative. As Marx noted, "History is not like some individual person, which uses men to achieve its ends. History is nothing but the actions of men in pursuit of their ends." So, individual characters do matter. Trump can be a useful reminder of that truism as we get students to explore their own historical moment, in light of other historical moments that Shakespeare, a keen student of history, was also aware of.

One way to gain insight and perspective into our own era is to note, as Charles McNulty does, that there are strong parallels between past ages and that of our own political situation, "Democratic pressures continually tested the ancient Republic, as the equilibrium between patricians and plebeians shifted. Today a similar contest for power is taking place between elites and everyday workers." What has been alarming but at the same time educational about the Trump rise is the fault lines that he exposed between the elites and the rest of us. Trump as a kind of cultural outsider understood in a way that many of those elites did not, that a good slice of the US despised their privileges and abhorred the policies they saw as favoring less deserving groups, such as immigrants and African Americans. To have effectively mounted a campaign that drilled home the anti-elitist message while flying around in his own 727 was not an easy trick to pull off.

- We might start the discussion of Trump and Shakespeare with that question. How can the Bard--the master artist of his time and ours help us to understand how Trump a billionaire businessman and deal-maker, with a shady past, manage to rise from reality TV show host to president?

Students might offer a variety of answers--well he was good on TV or on Twitter, he was able to use the email issue against Hilary, he was helped by the Russians and Comey etc. You might agree with all of that and still say we are missing one more reason. For me, it was his special talent to milk the politics of resentment to such a degree that Hillary Clinton, who came from more modest circumstances than Trump (who inherited from his father a sizeable fortune) was portrayed as the poster child of the elite, who because she had kept a private email server was somehow guilty of nefarious crimes.

He began to tap into the politics of resentment through an unusual route. Trump started out with exploiting the subtle racial resentment that he sensed was growing among a certain swath of white voters concerning the election of the first African American president, Barack Obama.

Othello

The key play here is, of course, *Othello* - one of the greatest tragedies, along with *Lear* and *Hamlet*, Shakespeare ever penned - that has a universal message regarding the way the so called "race card" can be played by the insecure to destroy not just individuals but relationships and entire communities.

For those of a certain generation, who saw advances by blacks in the 60s and 70s as threats to their own privileged status, Trump's voice leading the charge that Obama was not a legitimate American president, was exactly the tonic. Demanding to see Obama's full birth certificate did two things for him--it positioned him nationally as a right-wing leader who had the courage to express his unpopular views and it put him in the same presidential arena as Obama. How does this connect with Shakespeare? Through *Othello* Shakespeare that explores in some depth racial resentment and the subtle ways machiavellian-minded protagonists like Iago can play the race game.

Iago in one of his famous soliloquy sets out his plan based on an unproven and paranoid notion that his wife has slept with Othello

I hate the Moor:
And it is thought abroad, that 'twixt my sheets
He has done my office: I know not if't be true;
But I, for mere suspicion in that kind,
Will do as if for surety. He holds me well;
The better shall my purpose work on him.
Cassio's a proper man: let me see now:
To get his place and to plume up my will
In double knavery--How, how? Let's see:--

Iago`s actions resembles Trump in respect to his ability to tell big awful lies that profoundly damage other people and to use those around him to advance his plans. Iago is also a consummate actor capable of looking into anyone's eyes and telling an appalling lie. Trump's birther lie lasted five years and when he was finally pressured to drop it after he had won the nomination, he gave no apology or explanation. Instead, as this Politico report reminds us, put the blame on Hillary Clinton. Iago interestingly does not apologize for his slander and when asked for an explanation of his villainy merely says,

Demand me nothing: what you know, you know:
From this time forth I never will speak word.

We could go further to examine Trump and Iago's motivations by asking our students why both of them fail to account for their behavior. There are three negations in Iago's short crisp and last summation of who he is--"Demand me nothing", "What you know you know" and "I will never speak a word." Is Shakespeare pointing to Iago's essential nihilism. The vacuity of his motives is echoed by the concision of the sentence--its lack of articles--the repetition of "know" leading us to a semantic dead end. The words are spat out and we are left to sort out their meaning. Iago does not believe that the fundamental point of communication is to share truth about the world.

- We can ask our class whether they can find any similarities between Iago's non-confessional moment with Trump's own last words in the birther controversy,

"Hillary Clinton started the 'birther' controversy, I finished it. Barack Obama was born in the United States, period. Now we all want to get back to making the United States great again."

He completes his statement with what might be worse than a negation--an outright lie that Hillary Clinton started the birther controversy and then continues to go back into campaign mode as though his declaring the issue over. Isn't this, you may ask them, Trump's version of "what you know you know" --demand me nothing. From this time forth I will never speak another word?

King Lear

The birther movement that Trump instigated and kept alive for five years was the first shot in the campaign to move from a racially tolerant and diverse society to one under Trump that was far less so. We now no longer much talk about that bizarrely dark chapter in the history of Trump's rise because, like all of Shakespeare's villains, their job is to keep the action moving. If we had stopped the action at Macbeth or Richard III first crimes, we would feel shortchanged. So, the next set of questions to ask is what sort of ruthless character are we dealing with here that has so little regard for the truth that he surrounds himself with family members whom he rewards with top jobs in his administration as if he were a royal?

Trump's brand is intimately connected with family and with demanding loyalty, not just from them but from an entire entourage of cabinet members and members of his inner circle. Like Lear he has a hard time separating family business from political and understanding the difference between showy presentations and real loyalty. In an echo of KIng Lear's first scene, according to this New York Times report, he un-embarrassedly encouraged his cabinet members to provide him with declarations of admiration.

"The greatest privilege of my life is to serve as vice president to the president who's keeping his word to the American people," Mike Pence said, starting things off.
"I am privileged to be here — deeply honored — and I want to thank you for your commitment to the American workers," said Alexander Acosta, the secretary of labor.
Sonny Perdue, the agriculture secretary, had just returned from Mississippi and had a message to deliver. "They love you there," he offered, grinning across the antique table at Mr. Trump.
Reince Priebus, the chief of staff whose job insecurity has been the subject of endless speculation, outdid them all, telling the president — and the assembled news cameras — "We thank you for the opportunity and the blessing to serve your agenda."

- Students might be asked to question what would Trump's reaction have been if one of the cabinet members or children (Ivanka perhaps?) had said something similar to Cordelia`s reply to Lear's question

Which of you shall we say doth love us most?
That we our largest bounty may extend

And she had answered, a plain old "Nothing, my lord."

(Would Trump have subjected her to the same public humiliation that he dishes out to Cordelia--basically disowning them?

> Here I disclaim all my paternal care,
> Propinquity and property of blood,
> And as a stranger to my heart and me
> Hold thee, from this, for ever. The barbarous Scythian,
> Or he that makes his generation messes
> To gorge his appetite, shall to my bosom
> Be as well neighbour's, pitied, and relieved,
> As thou my sometime daughter.

We know Trump can be rash and impulsive but to this degree? Perhaps but let your students argue it out. By the same token can Trump's family members be as calculatingly evil as Goneril and Regan? Both have the same capacity that Trump has for both flattery and insult. They can turn on both in equal measure according to what the moment requires. In the highly theatrical setting of the demand for an oath of loyalty each tries to out-do the other in the flattery department. This is Goneril for example proclaiming her devotion

> Sir, I love you more than words can wield the matter;
> Dearer than eyesight, space, and liberty;
> Beyond what can be valued, rich or rare;
> No less than life, with grace, health, beauty, honour;
> As much as child e'er loved, or father found;
> A love that makes breath poor, and speech unable;
> Beyond all manner of so much I love you.

Compare that to one of Trump's over the top praise of French president Macron after insulting his country "The friendship between our two nations—and ourselves, I might add—are unbreakable." Trump, just like Lear, runs on flattery, both as a form of control of those around him - a way to emphasize that loyalty is a more important value than anything else - and to satisfy a childish need for reassurance that he is indeed as great a person as he imagines himself to be. It is no surprise that according to reports, , "President Donald Trump has a folder delivered to him twice a day that's full of positive headlines, tweets, interviews, and sometimes photographs of him on TV "looking powerful,"

- You might ask your students--whether they agree that Lear gains the same psychic rewards from both forms of flattery.

It is easier at this point of time to visualize Trump being forced from office than voluntarily giving up power in the manner of Lear. But we can visualize the way his family and coterie might respond to the loss of power and to what extent they will join forces against him. Will they be as cruel as Lear's daughters---casting him out of one of his mansions as they seek possession, or torturing one of his sycophants as Goneril recommends is done to Gloucester by removing his eyes?

Julius Caesar

Trump rose to power largely on the basis of his ability to get massive crowds excited about his Make America Great Again message. To better understand Trump's capacity to take control of the crowd, almost as if it were a living breathing animal we might use these two great plays as reference points.

Shakespeare, since the early English history plays, is interested in the power of language to move crowds and we should examine both *Julius Caesar* and *Corialanus* as dramatizations of the role that rhetoric and the crowd play in politics. In the former drama, after the conspiracy to kill Caesar, Brutus is, like any Roman Consul, compelled to justify his actions before the Roman citizenry.

His speech in Act lll is factual and he tries to level with the audience and only tepidly emotional, He offers a highly rational justification for his act--that he assassinated Rome's ruler not for any selfish reasons but because he was about to take away their freedoms. It was a patriotic decision to prevent a tyrant from taking control.

Students should examine the word choice "Respect", "honour" "wisdom" "ambition" . Brutus, who has a reputation as an honest servant of the people, makes a simple case. It is the sort of speech a Hillary Clinton would have given had she been so inclined to join a criminal conspiracy – dour, non-flashy and factual:

Be patient till the last.
Romans, countrymen, and lovers! hear me for my
cause, and be silent, that you may hear: believe me
for mine honour, and have respect to mine honour, that
you may believe: censure me in your wisdom, and
awake your senses, that you may the better judge.
If there be any in this assembly, any dear friend of
Caesar's, to him I say, that Brutus' love to Caesar
was no less than his. If then that friend demand
why Brutus rose against Caesar, this is my answer:

Then we have Antony take the stage--someone who has far more experience with much hotter rhetoric--the kind that Trump figured out a way to exploit.

Friends, Romans, countrymen, lend me your ears;
I come to bury Caesar, not to praise him.
The evil that men do lives after them;
The good is oft interred with their bones;
So let it be with Caesar. The noble Brutus
Hath told you Caesar was ambitious:
If it were so, it was a grievous fault,
And grievously hath Caesar answered it. ...

..You all did see that on the Lupercal
I thrice presented him a kingly crown,
Which he did thrice refuse: was this ambition?
Yet Brutus says he was ambitious;
And, sure, he is an honourable man.
I speak not to disprove what Brutus spoke,
But here I am to speak what I do know.
You all did love him once, not without cause:
What cause withholds you then, to mourn for him?

O judgment! thou art fled to brutish beasts,
And men have lost their reason. Bear with me;
My heart is in the coffin there with Caesar,
And I must pause till it come back to me.

Whereas Brutus`s speech is on the abstract side, Antony's is full of specificity and detail, designed to whip up the emotions. Anthony urges the audience to revisit Caesar's refusal of the crown and with subtle grace notes - for example note the use of the word "grievously" referencing both grief and an unjust bodily wound - and the play on words between ``Brutus`` and ``brutish`` and the calculated display of emotion as he simulates a mini- break down

Anthony then moves to describing, again with more specificity, how Caesar benefited Rome. He brought home more "captives" (slaves) for example that brought ransoms that filled the treasury. Caesar was so emotionally connected with Rome's poor that he cried for them. But like Trump he wants to hold the audience off just a few minutes longer from taking their revenge on one of the elites who betrayed them. If they would be patient, he has more to say and a few surprises. Anthony seems to anticipate the age of television where ratings flow from dramatic video --he has already secreted Caesar's will in his pocket and he will read it to them if they quieten down but he first has to tease them with the news they are about to receive,

Have patience, gentle friends, I must not read it;
It is not meet you know how Caesar loved you.
You are not wood, you are not stones, but men;
And, being men, bearing the will of Caesar,
It will inflame you, it will make you mad:
'Tis good you know not that you are his heirs;
For, if you should, O, what would come of it!

Of course, our response and that of the First citizens are identical

Read the will; we'll hear it, Antony;
You shall read us the will, Caesar's will.

Then we arrive at the hottest rhetoric that drives the crowd almost to the point of madness, as Antony reveals the money each Roman is going to receive and the walks and arbors that he has bequeathed to Rome.

O, pardon me, thou bleeding piece of earth,
That I am meek and gentle with these butchers!
Thou art the ruins of the noblest man
That ever lived in the tide of times...
..Blood and destruction shall be so in use
And dreadful objects so familiar
That mothers shall but smile when they behold
Their infants quartered with the hands of war;

Compare this to Trump's rhetoric about Hillary --the same meme - that the common people have been betrayed and sold out by a corrupt opposition that has carefully disguised itself as a friend of the people. Trump, like Anthony, has the patriotism and courage to reveal the true traitor. Note how Trump's words, like Anthony's, are carefully designed to inflame but he alone is there to protect them from the evils that his opponents threaten,

"We're going to renegotiate our disastrous trade deals and illegal immigration. Stop the massive inflow of refugees. Take care of our vets, our great vets. And we're going to repeal and replace Obamacare, 100 percent. That is a disaster. Premiums are soaring double digits in North Carolina, beyond anybody's wildest expectations. It's a disaster and you're -- and you know what's going on. Your country will be left with only one insurer. You're going to have nothing, everyone's leaving. And you have one insurer. You're going to have nobody. Obamacare if failing, we're going to repeal it and we're going to replace it.
(APPLAUSE)
Your jobs come back under a Trump administration. Your income goes up under a Trump administration. (APPLAUSE)
Your taxes go way down under a Trump administration.
(APPLAUSE)
You companies won't be leaving our country under a Trump administration, they'll be staying right here. And believe me, there are plenty of them right now negotiating to leave, I hate to tell you that.

These are the issues that we'll discuss at the next debate, which I look very much forward to.
(APPLAUSE)
Crooked Hillary is doing no more public events until after the debate. They say she's doing debate prep but really she's just resting, she's resting.
AUDIENCE: Lock her up! Lock her up! Lock her up!

Trump's level of anger here is palpable. Compare it to the middle of one of Hillary Clinton's stump speeches, Trump is not nearly as skilled a rhetorician as Antony. His vocabulary according to several reports is mostly at a 4th grade level. But he does know how to hone in on hot-button issues and to enrage the crowd in a way that can (and sometimes did) lead to violence. He perfected the speaking style over the course of many campaign rallies. As NBC reporter Katy Tur reports:

"Early on, they were kind of these rally speeches were a bit rambling and all over the place, to the point where even the people who were excited to see, they'd start walking out towards the end because they would sometimes go on for an hour-and-a-half. And there would be no real point; he'd just talk in circles. As he went on, he started to really hone his message. And he started to remember what lines worked. I believe he introduced "bomb the hell out of ISIS" at a New Hampshire rally early last fall. And it just got a huge, unbelievable roar from the crowd. And you could see he noted it. And he continued to do it from there going forward."

Hillary, in her stump speech by contrast, is factual but essentially unemotional. She is not playing for the camera so much as for history and her appeal is to a relatively comfortable middle-class audience that wants incremental not transformational change.

"We're going to make this economy grow but we're also going to make it fair. We're going to have more advanced manufacturing jobs. I think we made a mistake years ago when we eliminated what used to be called vocational education. We've got to return technical education to our high schools, our community colleges. There are right now more than a million jobs that can be filled by people who are machinists, computer designers, tool and die makers. But for whatever reason they haven't been given the chance to get that training. And maybe they've been told, you know what, the only future is to go to a great university like USF. Well, that is true for a lot of people, but it's not true for everybody, and we need to make the hard work that builds America the kind of great work with respect and purpose that is going to attract a new generation."

- After asking your students to review both speeches, ask your students which Shakespeare characters either of the 2016 candidates most resembles.
- Ask students to deliver their own speeches Brutus or Anthony style.

Coriolanus

Corialanus, like Trump, has an overwhelming sense of ego and pride--enough to fill more than a few skyscraper properties with his name synonymous with his brand of elite wealth plastered all over them. In the tragedy of the same name we are shown how how Caius-Martius, an ordinary Roman general, becomes Corialanus--his ego swollen after being awarded the name as the victor of the Battle of Corioli. While the play is not often taught in schools old copies might be dusted off because as Noah Millman suggests, the play which "takes place 2,500 years ago, in the early years of the Roman republic, and describes the banishment from Rome of its greatest military hero, who in exile allies with his greatest enemy to wreak vengeance on the city that spurned him, "could have been written this year."

Coriolanus is in at least two respects the opposite of Trump--Trump supposedly "loves" his voters, his largely white blue-collar base and the Roman warrior Coriolanus is contemptuous of them. The second major difference is that Coriolanus is a distinguished soldier, a battle-scarred warrior who makes a big deal of his personal sacrifices for Rome whereas Trump has the opposite claim to fame--he dodged the draft and built his empire on the back of his father's real estate fortune and ruthless greed and has preferred taking advantage of opportunities to enrich himself rather than sharing. So, what do they have in common? Several things. They are both outsiders who want power that they translate into personal admiration. They are men of action with a hot impulsive temper when things do not go their way. They both see politics as an act--a performance and a means to an end and are willing to do and say radical things if their main needs for fame and success are not met in the ways they determine. Setting up the task of comparing the two characters could be a useful way to start a discussion of the play.

Like Trump, Coriolanus seizes upon his moment in history to capitalize on his brand--the one that brooks no enemies that is ruthless in battle and brutally honest with the plebeians in a way that the corrupt politicians of this time cannot be. Both feel self-empowered by their sense of self-importance, boosted beyond all measure, by being validated in the public eyes to cast judgments on anyone and everyone who displeases them or, in their eyes, falls short of the mark. The attitude of being above the fray is so extreme that it causes Brutus to remark,

"You speak of' the people,
As if you were a god to punish, not
A man of their infirmity"

Somewhat like Trump, Coriolanus wins the people over by insulting them and thereby holding true to his brand of unrelenting honesty. He believes, like Trump, he is providing them with a gift

Why in this woolvish toge should I stand here,
To beg of Hob and Dick, that do appear,
Their needless vouches? Custom calls me to't:
What custom wills, in all things should we do't,
The dust on antique time would lie unswept,
And mountainous error be too highly heapt
For truth to o'er-peer. Rather than fool it so,
Let the high office and the honour go
To one that would do thus. I am half through;
The one part suffer'd, the other will I do.

What drives the crowd and Trump into an ardent but essentially sick relationship is their mutual hatred and anger about the elites.

"Care for us?" the people cry. "They ne'er cared for us yet. Suffer us to famish, and their storehouses crammed with grain; make edicts for usury, to support usurers: repeal daily any wholesome act established against the rich, and provide more piercing statutes daily, to chain up and restrain the poor. If the wars eat us not up, they will: and there's all the love they bear us."

There is also a hint that they might secretly identify with Coriolanus--just as for Trump supporters he is their idea of the way they would behave if they had a billion or more dollars to their name. As Menenius observes, there may be some hypocrisy involved:

"You talk of pride: O that you could turn your eyes toward the napes of your necks, and make but an interior survey of your good selves!"

For both Coriolanus and Trump and one might argue their supporters, the world is binary. They live by a simple code --you are or against me great individuals win against the odds. Winning is everything --losers need to leave the game for those blessed with the right combination of willpower and ruthless energy. How the winning is achieved is secondary to the fact that an opponent has been felled. It is no coincidence that Trump is associated with competitive (but ironically fixable games) -pro wrestling, Beauty pageants and the Apprentice. His trademark slogan is "You're Fired." The losers are supposed to walk off the stage with their head in their hands and never to appear again, the winners are green lighted for more action and aggression. The essence of both their characters is action not words--so it is perfectly in character for Coriolanus, upset by his treatment by the plebeians to abandon the city and to join its enemies, the Volscians, to lead an attack on it.

Students need to be reminded in all this that making comparisons between characters in fiction and people in real life is always a perilous business. Characters in fiction are fully formed and as the product of someone's artistic imagination consistent and more fully understandable than their human counterparts. Characters in the real world are often more contradictory and much less finished than in works of art. They also are capable of action and surprise whereas characters in fiction are dead on the page. Notwithstanding, students should be able to engage in a different more urgent way with some of the parallels between Trump and Shakespeare's characters and thereby deepen their own understanding of the plays.

Chapter 7: Framing Trump

One of the reasons to study the humanities is to gain a better understanding of language--how it can be used, misused and manipulated. What is surprising about Trump, who has never it seems read a serious book from cover to cover in his life, is the sophistication of his understanding about how to use language to persuade people as opposed to most of his rivals who actually bothered to study many of the Humanities so called required books.

This chapter comes last because any reader of this book must now be aware of the way Trump has mastered how to use language to advance his own political agenda. We, along with our students, may say that he is that not like any other politician? The answer is yes and no. Yes, because clearly every politician expresses a particular worldview through his or her choice of words. No, because Trump is not like a normal politician, in that he has, more than any other modern politician, mastered the art of social media--(specifically Twitter) and has thus extended his ability to have his way of seeing the world enter more everyday discussions and TV commentary than any other contemporary politician. Additionally, his mastery of Twitter has allowed him to become more adept at framing issues than most, if not all, contemporary politicians.

We cannot understand Trump's mastery of message without the help of George Lakoff, a Berkeley sociolinguist, and his ideas about framing. In many of his books and articles Lakoff returns to a few salient points regarding two distinct world views - the progressive and the conservative. [16]First, the progressive view is based around the nurturant family:

[16] http://www.berkeley.edu/news/media/releases/2003/10/27_lakoff.shtml

"The progressive worldview is modeled on a nurturant parent family. Briefly, it assumes that the world is basically good and can be made better and that one must work toward that. Children are born good; parents can make them better. Nurturing involves empathy, and the responsibility to take care of oneself and others for whom we are responsible. On a larger scale, specific policies follow, such as governmental protection in form of a social safety net and government regulation, universal education (to ensure competence, fairness), civil liberties and equal treatment (fairness and freedom), accountability (derived from trust), public service (from responsibility), open government (from open communication), and the promotion of an economy that benefits all and functions to promote these values, which are traditional progressive values in American politics".

The conservative worldview centers around "the strict father model" and it "..assumes that the world is dangerous and difficult and that children are born bad and must be made good. The strict father is the moral authority who supports and defends the family, tells his wife what to do, and teaches his kids right from wrong. The only way to do that is through painful discipline - physical punishment that by adulthood will become internal discipline. The good people are the disciplined people. Once grown, the self-reliant, disciplined children are on their own. Those children who remain dependent (who were spoiled, overly willful, or recalcitrant) should be forced to undergo further discipline or be cut free with no support to face the discipline of the outside world."

Lakoff's argument is that, in some way, all political debate is connected with these fundamental divides or frames and that specific arguments only stick with the electorate if they are connected with one of these frames or master narratives. The Republicans tend to be much better at this game than the Democrats. Lakoff suggests taking the 2004 Presidential election as a case in point. Republicans ran with the repetition of the idea ad nauseum that Kerry was "a flip-flopper", someone who was only pretending to seem centrist but was in reality swinging from one side of the left of the political spectrum to the other. As Matt Bai points out, "The smartest ad of the campaign may have been the one that showed Kerry windsurfing, expertly gliding back and forth, back and forth." In contrast, as Bai also makes clear, "Democrats. presented a litany of different complaints about Bush, depending on the day and the backdrop; he was a liar, a corporate stooge, a spoiled rich kid, a reckless warmonger. But they never managed to tie them all into a single, unifying image that voters could associate with the president. As a result, none of them stuck. Bush was attacked. Kerry was framed."

Democrats are on the losing side of so many of these framing issues. Take that of taxes--they have been successfully framed by the Republicans as an unjust burden --and so the phrase "tax relief" has entered into everyone's vocabulary. As Bai states it, "If Democrats start to talk about their own "tax relief" plan, Lakoff says, they have conceded the point that taxes are somehow an unfair burden rather than making the case that they are an investment in the common good. The argument is lost before it begins."

In Lakoff's view the Republicans have "done something that's perfectly legal. What they've done is find ways to set their frames into words over many years and have then repeated over and over again and have everybody say it the same way and get their journalists to repeat them, until they became part of normal English." Democrats, having been a majority party, for a long time did not feel they had the need to reframe their issues.

Of course, the idea that language and narrative matter in politics shouldn't really have come as a revelation to Washington Democrats. Bill Clinton had been an intuitive master of framing. As far back as 1992, Clinton's image of Americans who "worked hard and played by the rules," for instance, had perfectly evoked the metaphor of society as a contest that relied on fairness. And yet despite this, Democrats in Congress were remarkably slow to grasp this dimension of political combat. Having ruled Capitol Hill pretty comfortably for most of the past 60 years, Democrats had never had much reason to think about calibrating their language in order to sell their ideas.

"I can describe, and I've always been able to describe, what Republicans stand for in eight words, and the eight words are lower taxes, less government, strong defense and family values," Dorgan, who runs the Democratic Policy Committee in the Senate, told me recently. "We Democrats, if you ask us about one piece of that, we can meander for 5 or 10 minutes in order to describe who we are and what we stand for. And frankly, it just doesn't compete very well. I'm not talking about the policies. I'm talking about the language."

Students might be asked what kind of parental/rhetorical style does Trump represent? That is an easy one after reading extracts from this speech he gave in August around the hot-button issue of immigration reform in Phoenix, Arizona on August 31st to a packed rally of supporters:

Have your students read this abbreviated version and identify the various memes (mini-narratives) that Lakoff identifies. To simplify things, we can review a few of them:

1) Father deeply protective of his nation (not just the family) and angry that because of lax laws and permissive weak office holders, the nation is now placed in peril.

   Trump Storyline: Father as action hero--superman upset and ready to take action (getting his cape ready)

2) Those from other countries are fundamentally different from native born Americans. Individual crimes committed by foreigners who illegally entered the country are representative of a more general danger that the elites are ignoring. Illegal immigrants are harming our country

   Trump Storyline: Only superman has the insight and courage to take action (has his cape on)

3) We are facing a crisis. There are only two paths to solve it--capitulation to the forces of evil, who are in conspiracy with the elites to harm you or follow my father tough solution.

   Trump Storyline: I am pure and above the kind of corruption that has led the elites to make the wrong unpatriotic choices. They won't take action but I will (has his gloves on and ready to lift off to fight)_

You can ask your students to highlight (even use color coded highlighters) any of these memes in the speech (see Appendix).

Questions to ask students

1. Why do you think Trump begins and ends his speech with "I love you"? Why is that important to do rhetorically?
2. Why does Trump portray the immigration issue in a binary way? Are there other possible ways to control immigration other than building a wall?
3. What does adding all the graphic information about awful crimes committed by illegal immigrants do to the discussion. Does it serve to throw light or just more heat on the issue?
4. Examine the loaded phrases Trump uses – eg. "gross dereliction of duty". What are some other heated phrases.? What is the point of using the phrase "Trojan horse" ? What is Trump trying to signal but does not want to put into words?

Once students are aware of the way the Strict father, Permissive Mother game is played you can either give them more practice at spotting the tricks (some other Strict father speeches are included in the Appendix) or ask them to write their own strict father speeches. But there should be room to discuss and debate how far Trump pushes on the various memes to generate the anger and resentment that fueled his campaign. Unlike Reagan and Bush, Trump makes everything personal. His enemies are conspiring against the American people, they are personal and Hillary is so far from serving your needs, she "meets only with donors and lobbyists" and so forth.

Lakoff sets out Trumps' tried and true techniques for dominating the debate:

"1. **Repetition.** Words are neurally linked to the circuits that determine their meaning. The more a word is heard, the more the circuit is activated and the stronger it gets, and so the easier it is to fire again. Trump repeats. Win. Win, Win. We're gonna win so much you'll get tired of winning.

2. **Framing**: `Crooked Hillary`. Framing Hillary as purposely and knowingly committing crimes for her own benefit, which is what a crook does. Repeating the charge of crookedness makes many people unconsciously think of her that way, even though she has been found to have been honest and legal by the thorough investigations of the right-wing Benghazi committee and the FBI (which found nothing to accuse her with, except missing the mark '(C)' in the body of 3 out of 110,000 emails).

3. **Grammar**: `Radical Islamic terrorists`: "Radical" puts Muslims on a linear scale and "terrorists" imposes a frame on the scale, suggesting that terrorism is built into the religion itself. The grammar suggests that there is something about Islam that involves terrorism. Imagine calling the Charleston gunman a "radical Republican terrorist."

Trump is aware of this to at least some extent. As he said to Tony Schwartz, the ghostwriter who wrote *The Art of the Deal* for him, "I call it truthful hyperbole. It's an innocent form of exaggeration — and it's a very effective form of promotion."

This is the basis for the Trumpian metaphor that Naming is Identifying. Thus, naming your enemies will allow you to identify correctly who they are, get to them, and so allow you to defeat them. Hence, just saying "radical Islamic terrorists" allows you to pick them out, get at them, and annihilate them. And conversely, if you don't say it, you won't be able to pick them out and annihilate them. Thus, a failure to use those words means that you are protecting those enemies — in this case Muslims, who you regard as potential terrorists because of their religion.

Lakoff contends that the Democrats lost the presidential election and other recent elections because they are playing essentially on Republican defined turf. Their maternal and nurturing frames are not allowed to work because the GOP has been so masterful at the game that many people's brain circuits, including those of the media, have essentially been hijacked. Progressives must, in Lakoff's view, stop playing defense and go on the offense in terms of stating clearly their worldviews and the applicable frames.

Let's do the same analysis to the progressive world view and pull apart its mythic elements. Here is Lakoff again:

"The progressive worldview is modeled on a nurturant parent family. Briefly, it assumes that the world is basically good and can be made better and that one must work toward that. Children are born good; parents can make them better. Nurturing involves empathy, and the responsibility to take care of oneself and others for whom we are responsible. On a larger scale, specific policies follow, such as governmental protection in form of a social safety net and government regulation, universal education (to ensure competence, fairness), civil liberties and equal treatment (fairness and freedom), accountability (derived from trust), public service (from responsibility), open government (from open communication), and the promotion of an economy that benefits all and functions to promote these values, which are traditional progressive values in American politics".

We are a good people with a diverse range of people and culture who throughout history have made wiser choices by being more inclusive and caring of each other

Hillary Story line--We need to make sure everyone is at the table including women and minorities whose contributions have been too often overlooked

Government is instituted to reduce unnecessary suffering and to make the playing field equal where there is inequalities of opportunities either in the present or caused by past historical injustices.

Hillary Storyline- Government needs to be expanded in times of crisis and need and we can do this because I represent a fundamentally an optimistic people who know what is morally right thing to do and what is not

America cannot shrink from making amends for past injustices and to care for the victims of growing inequality in society

Hillary storyline--I will continue to insist that Minorities and immigrants will continue to make advances in the society

Students can examine some of the ways this speech contrasts with Trump's. They are different in purpose--Trump was providing some red meat to his loyal base in a border state regarding an issue that they care about, namely immigration. Hillary is speaking on national TV to accept the Democratic nomination. Hillary, as far as I can tell, did not give a speech solely devoted to immigration. You might consider why. Hillary needed to give all of the democratic constituencies something to fight for and to unite the various wings of her party. But there was no large disagreement on the issue of immigration inside the Democratic Party, so she can feel fairly confident that the call mid-way through the Speech to enable the children of illegal immigrants (the so called "Dreamers") to stay in the country would be well supported. But notice that call has to be justified in terms of economic justice-they are already contributing to our country.

There is also something missing from Trump's speeches and clearly included in the Hillary speech- it is empathy for our fellow citizens. She refers to "our children" and "dreams that are within reach" Lakoff does not want Democrats to be afraid of the notion that government is the enemy of free enterprise--that they should somehow apologize for spending on government. Instead, he wants people to recognize that-the private sector has been successful to the degree that there have been investments in roads and bridges and public education. The private sector could not flourish, as it has done, Lakoff claims, without a real partnership with the public sector. Trump and the GOP demagogues who support him, would have us believe that unions are out for themselves rather than serving as the one last buffer against workers being reduced to disposable parts, without rights or employment protections. It cannot be said often enough, they gave us the 40 hour week and the weekend. How many of our students know this?

Questions to ask students

- Why do you think Trump begins and ends his speech with "I love you"? Why is that important to do rhetorically?
- Why does Trump portray the immigration issue in a binary way? Are there other possible ways to control immigration other than building a wall?
- What does adding all the graphic information about awful crimes committed by illegal immigrants do to the discussion. Does it serve to throw light or just more heat on the issue?
- Examine the loaded phrases Trump uses "gross dereliction of duty" what are some other heated phrases. What is the point of using the phrase "Trojan horse" ? What is Trump trying to signal but does not want to put into words?

Conclusion

As the Trump outrages mount we can choose two courses of action. One is to feel too numbed by their outrageousness to take action. The other is to conclude that the person holding the highest office in the land is unfit to perform his duties and that everything must be done to resist lest the pattern of erratic behavior leads to something more severe--for example a world war that he starts through pique or a willingness to challenge the next election results if he loses and rules as a dictator. We have not seen this movie before and we still do not know how it will end.

In the mean-time as educators we need to do what we can do to help our students understand what is happening to the country and how key values are being subverted by a president who has shown minimal respect for truth, right and wrong or fairness. The Trump presidency represents a test for all of us. A test for our country to see if we can survive the assault on democratic freedoms we hold dear, such as the first amendment, which today, as I write, he has threatened by taking away the licenses of those who, in his view, are printing untrue news stories. A test for us as citizens and as professional educators. People in 1930s Europe had a similar choice as to whether to resist, as Raul Hilberg stated, with respect to the Holocaust, [17]

"Many people . . . saw or heard something of the event. Those of them who lived in Adolf Hitler's Europe would have described themselves, with few exceptions, as bystanders. They were not "involved," not willing to hurt the victims and not wishing to be hurt by the perpetrators. . . . The Dutch were worried about their bicycles, the French about shortages, the Ukrainians about food, the Germans about air raids. All of these people thought of themselves as victims, be it of war, or oppression, or "fate.""

In contrast there were some who stood up. As Elie Wiesel wrote[18],

---

[17] Facing History and Ourselves, Bystanders and Upstanders, https://www.facinghistory.org/resource-library/decision-making-times-injustice/holocaust-bystanders-upstanders

[18] Facing History and Ourselves, The Holocaust: Bystanders and Upstanders, https://www.facinghistory.org/resource-library/decision-making-times-injustice/holocaust-bystanders-upstanders

"Let us not forget, after all, that there is always a moment when the moral choice is made. Often because of one story or one book or one person, we are able to make a different choice, a choice for humanity, for life. And so we must know these good people who helped Jews during the Holocaust. We must learn from them, and in gratitude and hope, we must remember them."

Yes, we are not near another Holocaust. Trump is not Hitler but as someone who seems never to have read a book and with no understanding of history, he is repeating mistakes from which the world has barely started recovering.

Further Reading

Language and Propaganda

Lakoff, George, Don't Think Of An Elephant!/ How Democrats And Progressives Can Win, Chelsea Green 2005

McChesney, Robert, Rich Media, Poor Democracy: Communication Politics in Dubious Times (2000; The New Press, 2015)

Orwell, George, Politics and the English Language, Penguin, 2013

Roberts-Miller, Patricia Demagoguery and Democracy, The Experiment Books, 2017

Herman, Edward and Chomsky, Noam, Manufacturing Consent: The Political Economy of the Mass Media (Pantheon, 1988)

Stanley Jason, How Propaganda Works, Princeton, 2017

Race

Baldwin, James The Fire Next Time (Dial Press, 1963).

Coates, Ta-Nehisi , "On Homecomings," The Atlantic, May 9, 2016.

Douglass, Frederick, "The Meaning of July Fourth for the Negro," speech, July 5, 1852.

Secondary Readings

Hochschild, Arlie, Strangers in Their Own Land: Anger and Mourning on the American Right, The New Press, 2016

Kristof, Nicholas, "When Whites Just Don't Get It," New York Times, August 30, 2014

Michael Tesler, "Views about Race Mattered More in Electing Trump than Obama," Washington Post, November 22, 2016

Authoritarianism

Arendt, Hannah, The Origins of Totalitarianism, Harcourt, 1973

Synder, Timothy, On Tyranny: Twenty Lessons from the Twentieth Century, Tim Duggan Books 2017

Shirer, W., The Rise and Fall of the Third Reich, Rosetta Books, 2011

Taub, Amanda "The Rise of American Authoritarianism," Vox, March 1, 2016

Fictional Treatments

Lewis, Sinclair, It Can't Happen Here, Signet Books, 2014

Orwell, George, Animal Farm

Roth, Philip, The Plot Against America, Vintage Books, 2005

Political Analysis

Frank, Thomas, Listen Liberal, Or, What Ever Happened to the Party of the People? (Metropolitan Books/Henry Holt & Company) 2017

Packer, George, The Unwinding: An Inner History of the New America Paperback – March 4, 2014

Tesler, Michael and John Sides. "How Political Science Helps Explain the Rise of Trump: Most Voters Aren't Ideologues," Washington Post, March 2, 2016.

APPENDIX

Donald Trump's August 2016 Speech in Phoenix (transcript)[19]

TRUMP: Wow. Thank you. That's a lot of people, Phoenix, that's a lot of people.

(APPLAUSE)

Thank you very much.

Thank you, Phoenix. I am so glad to be back in Arizona.

(APPLAUSE)

The state that has a very, very special place in my heart. I love people of Arizona and together we are going to win the White House in November.

(APPLAUSE)

Now, you know this is where it all began for me. Remember that massive crowd also? So, I said let's go and have some fun tonight. We're going to Arizona, O.K.?

This will be a little bit different. This won't be a rally speech, per se. Instead, I'm going to deliver a detailed policy address on one of the greatest challenges facing our country today, illegal immigration.

(APPLAUSE)

I've just landed having returned from a very important and special meeting with the president of Mexico, a man I like and respect very much. And a man who truly loves his country, Mexico.

---

[19] https://www.nytimes.com/2016/09/02/us/politics/transcript-trump-immigration-speech.html

And, by the way, just like I am a man who loves my country, the United States.

(APPLAUSE)

We agree on the importance of ending the illegal flow of drugs, cash, guns, and people across our border, and to put the cartels out of business.

(APPLAUSE)

We also discussed the great contributions of Mexican-American citizens to our two countries, my love for the people of Mexico, and the leadership and friendship between Mexico and the United States. It was a thoughtful and substantive conversation and it will go on for awhile. And, in the end we're all going to win. Both countries, we're all going to win.

This is the first of what I expect will be many, many conversations. And in a Trump administration we're going to go about creating a new relationship between our two countries, but it's going to be a fair relationship. We want fairness.

(APPLAUSE)

But to fix our immigration system, we must change our leadership in Washington and we must change it quickly. Sadly, sadly there is no other way. The truth is our immigration system is worse than anybody ever realized. But the facts aren't known because the media won't report on them. The politicians won't talk about them and the special interests spend a lot of money trying to cover them up because they are making an absolute fortune. That's the way it is.

Today, on a very complicated and very difficult subject, you will get the truth. The fundamental problem with the immigration system in our country is that it serves the needs of wealthy donors, political activists and powerful, powerful politicians. It's all you can do. Thank you. Thank you.

(APPLAUSE)

Let me tell you who it does not serve. It does not serve you the American people. Doesn't serve you. When politicians talk about immigration reform, they usually mean the following: amnesty, open borders, lower wages. Immigration reform should mean something else entirely. It should mean improvements to our laws and policies to make life better for American citizens.

(APPLAUSE)

Thank you. But if we're going to make our immigration system work, then we have to be prepared to talk honestly and without fear about these important and very sensitive issues. For instance, we have to listen to the concerns that working people, our forgotten working people, have over the record pace of immigration and it's impact on their jobs, wages, housing, schools, tax bills and general living conditions.

These are valid concerns expressed by decent and patriotic citizens from all backgrounds, all over. We also have to be honest about the fact that not everyone who seeks to join our country will be able to successfully assimilate. Sometimes it's just not going to work out. It's our right, as a sovereign nation, to chose immigrants that we think are the likeliest to thrive and flourish and love us.

(APPLAUSE)

Then there is the issue of security. Countless innocent American lives have been stolen because our politicians have failed in their duty to secure our borders and enforce our laws like they have to be enforced. I have met with many of the great parents who lost their children to sanctuary cities and open borders. So many people, so many, many people. So sad. They will be joining me on this stage in a little while and I look forward to introducing, these are amazing, amazing people.

Countless Americans who have died in recent years would be alive today if not for the open border policies of this administration and the administration that causes this horrible, horrible thought process, called Hillary Clinton.

(APPLAUSE)

This includes incredible Americans like 21-year-old Sarah Root. The man who killed her arrived at the border, entered federal custody and then was released into the U.S., think of it, into the U.S. community under the policies of the White House Barack Obama and Hillary Clinton. Weak, weak policies. Weak and foolish policies.

He was released again after the crime, and now he's out there at large. Sarah had graduated from college with a 4.0, top student in her class one day before her death.

Also among the victims of the Obama-Clinton open-border policy was Grant Ronnebeck, a 21-year-old convenience store clerk and a really good guy from Mesa, Arizona. A lot of you have known about Grant.

He was murdered by an illegal immigrant gang member previously convicted of burglary, who had also been released from federal custody, and they knew it was going to happen again.

Another victim is Kate Steinle. Gunned down in the sanctuary city of San Francisco, by an illegal immigrant, deported five previous times. And they knew he was no good.

Then there is the case of 90-year-old Earl Olander, who was brutally beaten and left to bleed to death in his home, 90 years old and defenseless. The perpetrators were illegal immigrants with criminal records a mile long, who did not meet Obama administration standards for removal. And they knew it was going to happen.

In California, a 64-year-old Air Force veteran, a great woman, according to everybody that knew her, Marilyn Pharis, was sexually assaulted and beaten to death with a hammer. Her killer had been arrested on multiple occasions but was never, ever deported, despite the fact that everybody wanted him out.

A 2011 report from the Government Accountability Office found that illegal immigrants and other non-citizens, in our prisons and jails together, had around 25,000 homicide arrests to their names, 25,000.

On top of that, illegal immigration costs our country more than $113 billion a year. And this is what we get. For the money we are going to spend on illegal immigration over the next 10 years, we could provide one million at-risk students with a school voucher, which so many people are wanting.

While there are many illegal immigrants in our country who are good people, many, many, this doesn't change the fact that most illegal immigrants are lower skilled workers with less education, who compete directly against vulnerable American workers, and that these illegal workers draw much more out from the system than they can ever possibly pay back.

And they're hurting a lot of our people that cannot get jobs under any circumstances.

But these facts are never reported. Instead, the media and my opponent discuss one thing and only one thing, the needs of people living here illegally. In many cases, by the way, they're treated better than our vets.

Not going to happen anymore, folks. November 8th. Not going to happen anymore.

(APPLAUSE)

AUDIENCE: Trump! Trump! Trump!

The truth is, the central issue is not the needs of the 11 million illegal immigrants or however many there may be — and honestly we've been hearing that number for years. It's always 11 million. Our government has no idea. It could be three million. It could be 30 million. They have no idea what the number is.

Frankly our government has no idea what they're doing on many, many fronts, folks.

(APPLAUSE)

But whatever the number, that's never really been the central issue. It will never be a central issue. It doesn't matter from that standpoint. Anyone who tells you that the core issue is the needs of those living here illegally has simply spent too much time in Washington.

(APPLAUSE)

Only the out of touch media elites think the biggest problems facing America — you know this, this is what they talk about, facing American society today is that there are 11 million illegal immigrants who don't have legal status. And, they also think the biggest thing, and you know this, it's not nuclear, and it's not ISIS, it's not Russia, it's not China, it's global warming.

To all the politicians, donors, and special interests, hear these words from me and all of you today. There is only one core issue in the immigration debate, and that issue is the well being of the American people.

(APPLAUSE)

Nothing even comes a close second. Hillary Clinton, for instance, talks constantly about her fears that families will be separated, but she's not talking about the American families who have been permanently separated from their loved ones because of a preventable homicide, because of a preventable death, because of murder.

No, she's only talking about families who come here in violation of the law. We will treat everyone living or residing in our country with great dignity. So important.

We will be fair, just, and compassionate to all, but our greatest compassion must be for our American citizens.

(APPLAUSE)

Thank you.

President Obama and Hillary Clinton have engaged in gross dereliction of duty by surrendering the safety of the American people to open borders, and you know it better than anybody right here in Arizona. You know it.

President Obama and Hillary Clinton support sanctuary cities. They support catch and release on the border. They support visa overstays. They support the release of dangerous, dangerous, dangerous, criminals from detention. And they support unconstitutional executive amnesty.

Hillary Clinton has pledged amnesty in her first 100 days, and her plan will provide Obamacare, Social Security, and Medicare for illegal immigrants, breaking the federal budget.

On top of that she promises uncontrolled, low-skilled immigration that continues to reduce jobs and wages for American workers, and especially for African-American and Hispanic workers within our country. Our citizens.

Most incredibly, because to me this is unbelievable, we have no idea who these people are, where they come from. I always say Trojan horse. Watch what's going to happen, folks. It's not going to be pretty.

This includes her plan to bring in 620,000 new refugees from Syria and that region over a short period of time. And even yesterday, when you were watching the news, you saw thousands and thousands of people coming in from Syria. What is wrong with our politicians, our leaders if we can call them that. What the hell are we doing?

(APPLAUSE)

Hard to believe. Hard to believe. Now that you've heard about Hillary Clinton's plan, about which she has not answered a single question, let me tell you about my plan. And do you notice...

(APPLAUSE)

And do you notice all the time for weeks and weeks of debating my plan, debating, talking about it, what about this, what about that. They never even mentioned her plan on immigration because she doesn't want to get into the quagmire. It's a tough one, she doesn't know what she's doing except open borders and let everybody come in and destroy our country by the way.

(APPLAUSE)

While Hillary Clinton meets only with donors and lobbyists, my plan was crafted with the input from Federal Immigration offices, very great people. Among the top immigration experts anywhere in this country, who represent workers, not corporations, very important to us.

I also worked with lawmakers, who've led on this issue on behalf of American citizens for many years. And most importantly I've met with the people directly impacted by these policies. So important.

Number one, are you ready? Are you ready?

(APPLAUSE)

We will build a great wall along the southern border.

(APPLAUSE)

AUDIENCE: Build the wall! Build the wall! Build the wall!

And Mexico will pay for the wall.

(APPLAUSE)

One hundred percent. They don't know it yet, but they're going to pay for it. And they're great people and great leaders but they're going to pay for the wall.

On day one, we will begin working on an impenetrable, physical, tall, power, beautiful southern border wall.

(APPLAUSE)

We will use the best technology, including above and below ground sensors that's the tunnels. Remember that, above and below.

(APPLAUSE)

Above and below ground sensors. Towers, aerial surveillance and manpower to supplement the wall, find and dislocate tunnels and keep out criminal cartels and Mexico you know that, will work with us. I really believe it. Mexico will work with us. I absolutely believe it. And especially after meeting with their wonderful, wonderful president today. I really believe they want to solve this problem along with us, and I'm sure they will.

(APPLAUSE)

Number two, we are going to end catch and release. We catch them, oh go ahead. We catch them, go ahead.

(APPLAUSE)

Under my administration, anyone who illegally crosses the border will be detained until they are removed out of our country and back to the country from which they came.

(APPLAUSE)

And they'll be brought great distances. We're not dropping them right across. They learned that. President Eisenhower. They'd drop them across, right across, and they'd come back. And across.

Then when they flew them to a long distance, all of a sudden that was the end. We will take them great distances. But we will take them to the country where they came from, O.K.?

Number three. Number three, this is the one, I think it's so great. It's hard to believe, people don't even talk about it. Zero tolerance for criminal aliens. Zero. Zero.

(APPLAUSE)

Zero. They don't come in here. They don't come in here.

According to federal data, there are at least two million, two million, think of it, criminal aliens now inside of our country, two million people criminal aliens. We will begin moving them out day one. As soon as I take office. Day one. In joint operation with local, state, and federal law enforcement.

Now, just so you understand, the police, who we all respect — say hello to the police. Boy, they don't get the credit they deserve. I can tell you. They're great people. But the police and law enforcement, they know who these people are.

They live with these people. They get mocked by these people. They can't do anything about these people, and they want to. They know who these people are. Day one, my first hour in office, those people are gone.

(APPLAUSE)

And you can call it deported if you want. The press doesn't like that term. You can call it whatever the hell you want. They're gone.

Beyond the two million, and there are vast numbers of additional criminal illegal immigrants who have fled, but their days have run out in this country. The crime will stop. They're going to be gone. It will be over.

(APPLAUSE)

They're going out. They're going out fast.

Moving forward. We will issue detainers for illegal immigrants who are arrested for any crime whatsoever, and they will be placed into immediate removal proceedings if we even have to do that.

We will terminate the Obama administration's deadly, and it is deadly, non-enforcement policies that allow thousands of criminal aliens to freely roam our streets, walk around, do whatever they want to do, crime all over the place.

That's over. That's over, folks. That's over.

Since 2013 alone, the Obama administration has allowed 300,000 criminal aliens to return back into United States communities. These are individuals encountered or identified by ICE, but who were not detained or processed for deportation because it wouldn't have been politically correct.

My plan also includes cooperating closely with local jurisdictions to remove criminal aliens immediately. We will restore the highly successful Secure Communities Program. Good program. We will expand and revitalize the popular 287(g) partnerships, which will help to identify hundreds of thousands of deportable aliens in local jails that we don't even know about.

Both of these programs have been recklessly gutted by this administration. And those were programs that worked.

This is yet one more area where we are headed in a totally opposite direction. There's no common sense, there's no brain power in our administration by our leader, or our leaders. None, none, none.

On my first day in office I am also going to ask Congress to pass Kate's Law, named for Kate Steinle...

(APPLAUSE)

... to ensure that criminal aliens convicted of illegal reentry receive strong mandatory minimum sentences. Strong.

(APPLAUSE)

And then we get them out.

Another reform I'm proposing is the passage of legislation named for Detective Michael Davis and Deputy Sheriff Danny Oliver, two law enforcement officers recently killed by a previously deported illegal immigrant.

The Davis-Oliver bill will enhance cooperation with state and local authorities to ensure that criminal immigrants and terrorists are swiftly, really swiftly, identified and removed. And they will go face, believe me. They're going to go.

We're going to triple the number of ICE deportation officers.

(APPLAUSE)

Within ICE I am going to create a new special deportation task force focused on identifying and quickly removing the most dangerous criminal illegal immigrants in America who have evaded justice just like Hillary Clinton has evaded justice, O.K.?

(APPLAUSE)

Maybe they'll be able to deport her.

(APPLAUSE)

The local police who know every one of these criminals, and they know each and every one by name, by crime, where they live, they will work so fast. And our local police will be so happy that they don't have to be abused by these thugs anymore.

There's no great mystery to it, they've put up with it for years, and now finally we will turn the tables and law enforcement and our police will be allowed to clear up this dangerous and threatening mess.

We're also going to hire 5,000 more Border Patrol agents.

(APPLAUSE)

Who gave me their endorsement, 16,500 gave me their endorsement.

And put more of them on the border instead of behind desks which is good. We will expand the number of border patrol stations significantly.

I've had a chance to spend time with these incredible law enforcement officers, and I want to take a moment to thank them. What they do is incredible.

(APPLAUSE)

And getting their endorsement means so much to me. More to me really than I can say. Means so much. First time they've ever endorsed a presidential candidate.

Number four, block funding for sanctuary cities. We block the funding. No more funds.

(APPLAUSE)

We will end the sanctuary cities that have resulted in so many needless deaths. Cities that refuse to cooperate with federal authorities will not receive taxpayer dollars, and we will work with Congress to pass legislation to protect those jurisdictions that do assist federal authorities. Number five, cancel unconstitutional executive orders and enforce all immigration laws.

(APPLAUSE)

We will immediately terminate President Obama's two illegal executive amnesties in which he defied federal law and the Constitution to give amnesty to approximately five million illegal immigrants, five million.

(BOOING)

And how about all the millions that are waiting on line, going through the process legally? So unfair.

Hillary Clinton has pledged to keep both of these illegal amnesty programs, including the 2014 amnesty which has been blocked by the United States Supreme Court. Great.

Clinton has also pledged to add a third executive amnesty. And by the way, folks, she will be a disaster for our country, a disaster in so many other ways.

And don't forget the Supreme Court of the United States. Don't forget that when you go to vote on November 8. And don't forget your Second Amendment. And don't forget the repeal and replacement of Obamacare.

(APPLAUSE)

And don't forget building up our depleted military. And don't forget taking care of our vets. Don't forget our vets. They have been forgotten.

(APPLAUSE)

Clinton's plan would trigger a constitutional crisis unlike almost anything we have ever seen before. In effect, she would be abolishing the lawmaking powers of Congress in order to write her own laws from the Oval Office. And you see what bad judgment she has. She has seriously bad judgment.

(BOOING)

Can you imagine? In a Trump administration all immigration laws will be enforced, will be enforced. As with any law enforcement activity, we will set priorities. But unlike this administration, no one will be immune or exempt from enforcement. And ICE and Border Patrol officers will be allowed to do their jobs the way their jobs are supposed to be done.

(APPLAUSE)

Anyone who has entered the United States illegally is subject to deportation. That is what it means to have laws and to have a country. Otherwise we don't have a country.

Our enforcement priorities will include removing criminals, gang members, security threats, visa overstays, public charges. That is those relying on public welfare or straining the safety net along with millions of recent illegal arrivals and overstays who've come here under this current corrupt administration.

(APPLAUSE)

Number six, we are going to suspend the issuance of visas to any place where adequate screening cannot occur.

(APPLAUSE)

According to data provided by the Senate Subcommittee on Immigration, and the national interest between 9/11 and the end of 2014, at least 380 foreign born individuals were convicted in terror cases inside the United States. And even right now the largest number of people are under investigation for exactly this that we've ever had in the history of our country.

Our country is a mess. We don't even know what to look for anymore, folks. Our country has to straighten out. And we have to straighten out fast.

Morning Briefing
Get what you need to know to start your day in the United States, Canada and the Americas, delivered to your inbox.

Sign Up
SEE SAMPLE PRIVACY POLICY OPT OUT OR CONTACT US ANYTIME
The number is likely higher. But the administration refuses to provide this information, even to Congress. As soon as I enter office I am going to ask the Department of State, which has been brutalized by Hillary Clinton, brutalized.

(BOOING)

Homeland Security and the Department of Justice to begin a comprehensive review of these cases in order to develop a list of regions and countries from which immigration must be suspended until proven and effective vetting mechanisms can be put in place.

I call it extreme vetting right? Extreme vetting. I want extreme. It's going to be so tough, and if somebody comes in that's fine but they're going to be good. It's extreme.

And if people don't like it, we've got have a country folks. Got to have a country. Countries in which immigration will be suspended would include places like Syria and Libya. And we are going to stop the tens of thousands of people coming in from Syria. We have no idea who they are, where they come from. There's no documentation. There's no paperwork. It's going to end badly folks. It's going to end very, very badly.

For the price of resettling one refugee in the United States, 12 could be resettled in a safe zone in their home region. Which I agree with 100 percent. We have to build safe zones and we'll get the money from Gulf states. We don't want to put up the money. We owe almost $20 trillion. Doubled since Obama took office, our national debt.

But we will get the money from Gulf states and others. We'll supervise it. We'll build safe zones which is something that I think all of us want to see.

Another reform involves new screening tests for all applicants that include, and this is so important, especially if you get the right people. And we will get the right people. An ideological certification to make sure that those we are admitting to our country share our values and love our people.

(APPLAUSE)

Thank you. We're very proud of our country. Aren't we? Really? With all it's going through, we're very proud of our country. For instance, in the last five years, we've admitted nearly 100,000 immigrants from Iraq and Afghanistan. And these two countries according to Pew Research, a majority of residents say that the barbaric practice of honor killings against women are often or sometimes justified. That's what they say.

(APPLAUSE)

That's what they say. They're justified. Right? And we're admitting them to our country. Applicants will be asked their views about honor killings, about respect for women and gays and minorities. Attitudes on radical Islam, which our president refuses to say and many other topics as part of this vetting procedure. And if we have the right people doing it, believe me, very, very few will slip through the cracks. Hopefully, none.

(APPLAUSE)

Number seven, we will insure that other countries take their people back when they order them deported.

(APPLAUSE)

There are at least 23 countries that refuse to take their people back after they've been ordered to leave the United States. Including large numbers of violent criminals, they won't take them back. So we say, O.K., we'll keep them. Not going to happen with me, not going to happen with me.

(APPLAUSE)

Due to a Supreme Court decision, if these violent offenders cannot be sent home, our law enforcement officers have to release them into your communities.

(APPLAUSE)

And by the way, the results are horrific, horrific. There are often terrible consequences, such as Casey Chadwick's tragic death in Connecticut just last year. Yet despite the existence of a law that commands the secretary of state to stop issuing visas to these countries.

Secretary Hillary Clinton ignored this law and refused to use this powerful tool to bring nations into compliance. And, they would comply if we would act properly.

In other words, if we had leaders that knew what they were doing, which we don't.

The result of her misconduct was the release of thousands and thousands of dangerous criminal aliens who should have been sent home to their countries. Instead we have them all over the place. Probably a couple in this room as a matter of fact, but I hope not.

According to a report for the Boston Globe from the year 2008 to 2014 nearly 13,000 criminal aliens were released back into U.S. communities because their home countries would not, under any circumstances, take them back. Hard to believe with the power we have. Hard to believe.

We're like the big bully that keeps getting beat up. You ever see that? The big bully that keeps getting beat up.

These 13,000 releases occurred on Hillary Clinton's watch. She had the power and the duty to stop it cold, and she decided she would not do it.

(BOOING)

And Arizona knows better than most exactly what I'm talking about.

(APPLAUSE)

Those released include individuals convicted of killings, sexual assaults, and some of the most heinous crimes imaginable.

The Boston Globe writes that a Globe review of 323 criminals released in New England from 2008 to 2012 found that as many as 30 percent committed new offenses, including rape, attempted murder, and child molestation. We take them, we take them.

(BOOING)

Number eight, we will finally complete the biometric entry-exit visa tracking system which we need desperately.

(APPLAUSE)

For years Congress has required biometric entry-exit visa tracking systems, but it has never been completed. The politicians are all talk, no action, never happens. Never happens.

Hillary Clinton, all talk. Unfortunately when there is action it's always the wrong decision. You ever notice?

In my administration we will ensure that this system is in place. And, I will tell you, it will be on land, it will be on sea, it will be in air. We will have a proper tracking system.

Approximately half of new illegal immigrants came on temporary visas and then never, ever left. Why should they? Nobody's telling them to leave. Stay as long as you want, we'll take care of you.

Beyond violating our laws, visa overstays pose — and they really are a big problem — pose a substantial threat to national security. The 9/11 Commission said that this tracking system should be a high priority and would have assisted law enforcement and intelligence officials in August and September 2001 in conducting a search for two of the 9/11 hijackers that were in the United States on expired visas.

And you know what that would have meant, what that could have meant. Wouldn't that have been wonderful, right? What that could have meant.

Last year alone nearly half a million individuals overstayed their temporary visas. Removing these overstays will be a top priority of my administration.

(APPLAUSE)

If people around the world believe they can just come on a temporary visa and never, ever leave, the Obama-Clinton policy, that's what it is, then we have a completely open border, and we no longer have a country.

We must send a message that visa expiration dates will be strongly enforced.

Number nine, we will turn off the jobs and benefits magnet.

(APPLAUSE)

We will ensure that E-Verify is used to the fullest extent possible under existing law, and we will work with Congress to strengthen and expand its use across the country.

Immigration law doesn't exist for the purpose of keeping criminals out. It exists to protect all aspects of American life. The work site, the welfare office, the education system, and everything else.

That is why immigration limits are established in the first place. If we only enforced the laws against crime, then we have an open border to the entire world. We will enforce all of our immigration laws.

(APPLAUSE)

And the same goes for government benefits. The Center for Immigration Studies estimates that 62 percent of households headed by illegal immigrants use some form of cash or non-cash welfare programs like food stamps or housing assistance.

Tremendous costs, by the way, to our country. Tremendous costs. This directly violates the federal public charge law designed to protect the United States Treasury. Those who abuse our welfare system will be priorities for immediate removal.

(APPLAUSE)

Number 10, we will reform legal immigration to serve the best interests of America and its workers, the forgotten people. Workers. We're going to take care of our workers.

And by the way, and by the way, we're going to make great trade deals. We're going to renegotiate trade deals. We're going to bring our jobs back home. We're going to bring our jobs back home.

We have the most incompetently worked trade deals ever negotiated probably in the history of the world, and that starts with Nafta. And now they want to go TPP, one of the great disasters.

We're going to bring our jobs back home. And if companies want to leave Arizona and if they want to leave other states, there's going to be a lot of trouble for them. It's not going to be so easy. There will be consequence. Remember that. There will be consequence. They're not going to be leaving, go to another country, make the product, sell it into the United States, and all we end up with is no taxes and total unemployment. It's not going to happen. There will be consequences.

(APPLAUSE)

We've admitted 59 million immigrants to the United States between 1965 and 2015. Many of these arrivals have greatly enriched our country. So true. But we now have an obligation to them and to their children to control future immigration as we are following, if you think, previous immigration waves.

We've had some big waves. And tremendously positive things have happened. Incredible things have happened. To ensure assimilation we want to ensure that it works. Assimilation, an important word. Integration and upward mobility.

(APPLAUSE)

Within just a few years immigration as a share of national population is set to break all historical records. The time has come for a new immigration commission to develop a new set of reforms to our legal immigration system in order to achieve the following goals.

To keep immigration levels measured by population share within historical norms. To select immigrants based on their likelihood of success in U.S. society and their ability to be financially self-sufficient.

(APPLAUSE)

We take anybody. Come on in, anybody. Just come on in. Not anymore.

You know, folks, it's called a two-way street. It is a two-way street, right? We need a system that serves our needs, not the needs of others. Remember, under a Trump administration it's called America first. Remember that.

(APPLAUSE)

To choose immigrants based on merit. Merit, skill, and proficiency. Doesn't that sound nice? And to establish new immigration controls to boost wages and to ensure that open jobs are offered to American workers first. And that in particular African-American and Latino workers who are being shut out in this process so unfairly.

(APPLAUSE)

And Hillary Clinton is going to do nothing for the African-American worker, the Latino worker. She's going to do nothing. Give me your vote, she says, on November 8th. And then she'll say, so long, see you in four years. That's what it is.

She is going to do nothing. And just look at the past. She's done nothing. She's been there for 35 years. She's done nothing. And I say what do you have to lose? Choose me. Watch how good we're going to do together. Watch.

(APPLAUSE)

You watch. We want people to come into our country, but they have to come into our country legally and properly vetted, and in a manner that serves the national interest. We've been living under outdated immigration rules from decades ago. They're decades and decades old.

To avoid this happening in the future, I believe we should sunset our visa laws so that Congress is forced to periodically revise and revisit them to bring them up to date. They're archaic. They're ancient. We wouldn't put our entire federal budget on auto pilot for decades, so why should we do the same for the very, very complex subject of immigration?

So let's now talk about the big picture. These 10 steps, if rigorously followed and enforced, will accomplish more in a matter of months than our politicians have accomplished on this issue in the last 50 years. It's going to happen, folks. Because I am proudly not a politician, because I am not behold to any special interest, I've spent a lot of money on my campaign, I'll tell you. I write those checks. Nobody owns Trump.

I will get this done for you and for your family. We'll do it right. You'll be proud of our country again. We'll do it right. We will accomplish all of the steps outlined above. And, when we do, peace and law and justice and prosperity will prevail. Crime will go down. Border crossings will plummet. Gangs will disappear.

And the gangs are all over the place. And welfare use will decrease. We will have a peace dividend to spend on rebuilding America, beginning with our American inner cities. We're going to rebuild them, for once and for all.

For those here illegally today, who are seeking legal status, they will have one route and one route only. To return home and apply for reentry like everybody else, under the rules of the new legal immigration system that I have outlined above. Those who have left to seek entry —

Thank you.

Thank you. Thank you. Those who have left to seek entry under this new system — and it will be an efficient system — will not be awarded surplus visas, but will have to apply for entry under the immigration caps or limits that will be established in the future.TRUMP: We will break the cycle of amnesty and illegal immigration. We will break the cycle. There will be no amnesty.

(APPLAUSE)

Our message to the world will be this. You cannot obtain legal status or become a citizen of the United States by illegally entering our country. Can't do it.

(APPLAUSE)

This declaration alone will help stop the crisis of illegal crossings and illegal overstays, very importantly. People will know that you can't just smuggle in, hunker down and wait to be legalized. It's not going to work that way. Those days are over.

(APPLAUSE)

Importantly, in several years when we have accomplished all of our enforcement and deportation goals and truly ended illegal immigration for good, including the construction of a great wall, which we will have built in record time. And at a reasonable cost, which you never hear from the government.

(APPLAUSE)

And the establishment of our new lawful immigration system then and only then will we be in a position to consider the appropriate disposition of those individuals who remain.

That discussion can take place only in an atmosphere in which illegal immigration is a memory of the past, no longer with us, allowing us to weigh the different options available based on the new circumstances at the time.

(APPLAUSE)

Right now, however, we're in the middle of a jobs crisis, a border crisis and a terrorism crisis like never before. All energies of the federal government and the legislative process must now be focused on immigration security. That is the only conversation we should be having at this time, immigration security. Cut it off.

Whether it's dangerous materials being smuggled across the border, terrorists entering on visas or Americans losing their jobs to foreign workers, these are the problems we must now focus on fixing. And the media needs to begin demanding to hear Hillary Clinton's answer on how her policies will affect Americans and their security.

(APPLAUSE)

These are matters of life and death for our country and its people, and we deserve answers from Hillary Clinton. And do you notice, she doesn't answer.

She didn't go to Louisiana. She didn't go to Mexico. She was invited.

She doesn't have the strength or the stamina to make America great again. Believe me.

(APPLAUSE)

What we do know, despite the lack of media curiosity, is that Hillary Clinton promises a radical amnesty combined with a radical reduction in immigration enforcement. Just ask the Border Patrol about Hillary Clinton. You won't like what you're hearing.

The result will be millions more illegal immigrants; thousands of more violent, horrible crimes; and total chaos and lawlessness. That's what's going to happen, as sure as you're standing there.

This election, and I believe this, is our last chance to secure the border, stop illegal immigration and reform our laws to make your life better. I really believe this is it. This is our last time. November 8. November 8. You got to get out and vote on November 8.

(APPLAUSE)

It's our last chance. It's our last chance. And that includes Supreme Court justices and Second Amendment. Remember that. So I want to remind everyone what we're fighting for and who we are fighting for.

I am going to ask — these are really special people that I've gotten to know. I'm going to ask all of the "Angel Moms" to come join me on the stage right now.

These are amazing women.

(APPLAUSE)

These are amazing people.

(APPLAUSE)

AUDIENCE: USA! USA! USA!

I've become friends with so many. But Jamiel Shaw, incredible guy, lost his son so violently. Say just a few words about your child.

(SPEAKER'S VOICE): My son Ronald da Silva (ph) was murdered April 27, 2002 by an illegal alien who had been previously deported. And what so — makes me so outrageous is that we came here legally.

Thank you, Mr. Trump. I totally support you. You have my vote.

TRUMP: Thank you, thank you.

(SPEAKER'S VOICE): God bless you.

(APPLAUSE)

TRUMP: You know what? Name your child and come right by. Go ahead.

(SPEAKER'S VOICE): Laura Wilkerson. And my son was Joshua Wilkerson. He was murdered by an illegal in 2010. And I personally support Mr. Trump for our next president.

(APPLAUSE)

(SPEAKER'S VOICE): My name is Ruth Johnston Martin (ph). My husband was shot by an illegal alien. He fought the good fight but he took his last breath in 2002. And I support this man who's going to change this country for the better. God bless you.

(APPLAUSE)

(SPEAKER'S VOICE): My name Maureen Maloney (ph), and our son Matthew Denise (ph) was 23 years old when he was dragged a quarter of a mile to his death by an illegal alien, while horrified witnesses were banging on the truck trying to stop him.

(APPLAUSE)

(SPEAKER'S VOICE): Our son Matthew Denise, if Donald Trump were president in 2011, our son Matthew Denise and other Americans would be alive today.

(APPLAUSE)

(SPEAKER'S VOICE): Thank you. My name is Kathy Woods (ph). My son Steve (ph), a high school senior, 17 years old, went to the beach after a high school football game. A local gang came along, nine members. The cars were battered to — like war in Beirut. And all I can say is they murdered him and if Mr. Trump had been in office then the border would have been secure and our children would not be dead today.

(APPLAUSE)

(SPEAKER'S VOICE): Hi. My name is Brenda Sparks (ph), and my son is named Eric Zapeda (ph). He was raised by a legal immigrant from Honduras only to be murdered by an illegal in 2011. His murderer never did a second in handcuffs or jail. Got away with killing an American. So I'm voting for trump. And by the way, so is my mother.

(APPLAUSE)

(SPEAKER'S VOICE): My name is Dee Angle (ph). My cousin Rebecca Ann Johnston (ph), known as Becky, was murdered on January the 1st, 1989 in North Little Rock, Arkansas. Thank you. And if you don't vote Trump, we won't have a country. Trump all the way.

(APPLAUSE)

(SPEAKER'S VOICE): I'm Shannon Estes (ph). And my daughter Shaley Estes (ph), 22 years old, was murdered here in Phoenix last July 24 by a Russian who overstayed his visa. And vote Trump.

(APPLAUSE)

(SPEAKER'S VOICE): I'm Mary Ann Mendoza, the mother of Sergeant Brandon Mendoza, who was killed in a violent head-on collision in Mesa.

Thank you.

I want to thank Phoenix for the support you've always given me, and I want to tell you what. I'm supporting the man who will — who is the only man who is going to save our country, and what we our going to be leaving our children.

(APPLAUSE)

(SPEAKER'S VOICE): I'm Steve Ronnebeck, father of Grant Ronnebeck, 21 years old. Killed January 22, 2015 by an illegal immigrant who shot him in the face. I truly believe that Mr. Trump is going to change things. He's going to fight for my family, and he's going to fight for America.

(APPLAUSE)

TRUMP: These are amazing people, and I am not asking for their endorsement, believe me that. I just think I've gotten to know so many of them, and many more, from our group. But they are incredible people and what they're going through is incredible, and there's just no reason for it. Let's give them a really tremendous hand.

(APPLAUSE)

That's tough stuff, I will tell you. That is tough stuff. Incredible people.

So, now is the time for these voices to be heard. Now is the time for the media to begin asking questions on their behalf. Now is the time for all of us as one country, Democrat, Republican, liberal, conservative to band together to deliver justice, and safety, and security for all Americans.

Let's fix this horrible, horrible, problem. It can be fixed quickly. Let's our secure our border.

(APPLAUSE)

Let's stop the drugs and the crime from pouring into our country. Let's protect our social security and Medicare. Let's get unemployed Americans off the welfare and back to work in their own country.

This has been an incredible evening. We're going to remember this evening. November 8, we have to get everybody. This is such an important state. November 8 we have to get everybody to go out and vote.

We're going to bring — thank you, thank you. We're going to take our country back, folks. This is a movement. We're going to take our country back.

Thank you.

(APPLAUSE)

Thank you.

This is an incredible movement. The world is talking about it. The world is talking about it and by the way, if you haven't been looking to what's been happening at the polls over the last three or four days I think you should start looking. You should start looking.

(APPLAUSE)

Together we can save American lives, American jobs, and American futures. Together we can save America itself. Join me in this mission, we're going to make America great again.

Thank you. I love you. God bless you, everybody. God bless you. God bless you, thank you.

Nothing even comes a close second. Hillary Clinton, for instance, talks constantly about her fears that families will be separated, but she's not talking about the American families who have been permanently separated from their loved ones because of a preventable homicide, because of a preventable death, because of murder.

No, she's only talking about families who come here in violation of the law. We will treat everyone living or residing in our country with great dignity. So important.

We will be fair, just, and compassionate to all, but our greatest compassion must be for our American citizens.

Thank you.

Hillary Clinton Speech before the Democratic Convention, Philadelphia, July 2016[20]

Thank you! Thank you for that amazing welcome.

And Chelsea, thank you.

I'm so proud to be your mother and so proud of the woman you've become.

Thanks for bringing Marc into our family, and Charlotte and Aidan into the world.

And Bill, that conversation we started in the law library 45 years ago is still going strong.

It's lasted through good times that filled us with joy, and hard times that tested us.

And I've even gotten a few words in along the way.

On Tuesday night, I was so happy to see that my Explainer-in-Chief is still on the job.

I'm also grateful to the rest of my family and the friends of a lifetime.

To all of you whose hard work brought us here tonight.

And to those of you who joined our campaign this week.

And what a remarkable week it's been.

We heard the man from Hope, Bill Clinton.

And the man of Hope, Barack Obama.

---

[20] https://www.nytimes.com/2016/07/29/us/politics/hillary-clinton-dnc-transcript.html

America is stronger because of President Obama's leadership, and I'm better because of his friendship.

We heard from our terrific vice president, the one-and-only Joe Biden, who spoke from his big heart about our party's commitment to working people.

First lady Michelle Obama reminded us that our children are watching, and the president we elect is going to be their president, too.

And for those of you out there who are just getting to know Tim Kaine — you're soon going to understand why the people of Virginia keep promoting him: from City Council and mayor, to Governor, and now Senator.

He'll make the whole country proud as our Vice President.

And ... I want to thank Bernie Sanders.

Bernie, your campaign inspired millions of Americans, particularly the young people who threw their hearts and souls into our primary.

You've put economic and social justice issues front and center, where they belong.

And to all of your supporters here and around the country:

I want you to know, I've heard you.

Your cause is our cause.

Our country needs your ideas, energy, and passion.

That's the only way we can turn our progressive platform into real change for America.

We wrote it together — now let's go out there and make it happen together.

My friends, we've come to Philadelphia — the birthplace of our nation — because what happened in this city 240 years ago still has something to teach us today.

We all know the story.

But we usually focus on how it turned out — and not enough on how close that story came to never being written at all.

When representatives from 13 unruly colonies met just down the road from here, some wanted to stick with the King.

Some wanted to stick it to the king, and go their own way.

The revolution hung in the balance.

Then somehow they began listening to each other ... compromising ... finding common purpose.

And by the time they left Philadelphia, they had begun to see themselves as one nation.

That's what made it possible to stand up to a King.

That took courage.

They had courage.

Our Founders embraced the enduring truth that we are stronger together.

America is once again at a moment of reckoning.

Powerful forces are threatening to pull us apart.

Bonds of trust and respect are fraying.

And just as with our founders, there are no guarantees.

It truly is up to us.

We have to decide whether we all will work together so we all can rise together.

Our country's motto is e pluribus unum: out of many, we are one.

Will we stay true to that motto?

Well, we heard Donald Trump's answer last week at his convention.

He wants to divide us — from the rest of the world, and from each other.

He's betting that the perils of today's world will blind us to its unlimited promise.

He's taken the Republican Party a long way … from "Morning in America" to "Midnight in America."

He wants us to fear the future and fear each other.

Well, a great Democratic President, Franklin Delano Roosevelt, came up with the perfect rebuke to Trump more than eighty years ago, during a much more perilous time.

Now we are cleareyed about what our country is up against.

But we are not afraid.

We will rise to the challenge, just as we always have.

We will not build a wall.

Instead, we will build an economy where everyone who wants a good paying job can get one.

And we'll build a path to citizenship for millions of immigrants who are already contributing to our economy!

We will not ban a religion.

We will work with all Americans and our allies to fight terrorism.

There's a lot of work to do.

Too many people haven't had a pay raise since the crash.

There's too much inequality.

Too little social mobility.

Too much paralysis in Washington.

Too many threats at home and abroad.

But just look at the strengths we bring to meet these challenges.

We have the most dynamic and diverse people in the world.

We have the most tolerant and generous young people we've ever had.

We have the most powerful military.

The most innovative entrepreneurs.

The most enduring values. Freedom and equality, justice and opportunity.

We should be so proud that these words are associated with us. That when people hear them — they hear ... America.

So don't let anyone tell you that our country is weak.

We're not.

Don't let anyone tell you we don't have what it takes.

We do.

And most of all, don't believe anyone who says: "I alone can fix it."

Those were actually Donald Trump's words in Cleveland.

And they should set off alarm bells for all of us.

Really?

I alone can fix it?

Isn't he forgetting?

Troops on the front lines.

Police officers and fire fighters who run toward danger.

Doctors and nurses who care for us.

Teachers who change lives.

Entrepreneurs who see possibilities in every problem.

Mothers who lost children to violence and are building a movement to keep other kids safe.

He's forgetting every last one of us.

Americans don't say: "I alone can fix it."

We say: "We'll fix it together."

Remember: Our Founders fought a revolution and wrote a Constitution so America would never be a nation where one person had all the power.

Two hundred and forty years later, we still put our faith in each other.

Look at what happened in Dallas after the assassinations of five brave police officers.

Chief David Brown asked the community to support his force, maybe even join them.

And you know how the community responded?

Nearly 500 people applied in just 12 days.

That's how Americans answer when the call for help goes out.

20 years ago I wrote a book called "It Takes a Village." A lot of people looked at the title and asked, what the heck do you mean by that?

This is what I mean.

None of us can raise a family, build a business, heal a community or lift a country totally alone.

America needs every one of us to lend our energy, our talents, our ambition to making our nation better and stronger.

I believe that with all my heart.

That's why "Stronger Together" is not just a lesson from our history.

It's not just a slogan for our campaign.

It's a guiding principle for the country we've always been and the future we're going to build.

A country where the economy works for everyone, not just those at the top.

Where you can get a good job and send your kids to a good school, no matter what ZIP code you live in.

A country where all our children can dream, and those dreams are within reach.

Where families are strong ... communities are safe.

Democratic Convention Night 4: Analysis
How we provided real-time analysis of the final night of the Democratic National Convention, featuring Chelsea and Hillary Clinton.

And yes, love trumps hate.

That's the country we're fighting for.

That's the future we're working toward.

And so it is with humility ... determination ... and boundless confidence in America's promise ... that I accept your nomination for President of the United States!

Now, sometimes the people at this podium are new to the national stage.

As you know, I'm not one of those people.

I've been your first lady. Served 8 years as a Senator from the great sate of New York.

I ran for President and lost.

Then I represented all of you as secretary of State.

But my job titles only tell you what I've done.

They don't tell you why.

The truth is, through all these years of public service, the "service" part has always come easier to me than the "public" part.

I get it that some people just don't know what to make of me.

So let me tell you.

The family I'm from ... well, no one had their name on big buildings.

My family were builders of a different kind.

Builders in the way most American families are.

They used whatever tools they had — whatever God gave them — and whatever life in America provided — and built better lives and better futures for their kids.

My grandfather worked in the same Scranton lace mill for 50 years.

Because he believed that if he gave everything he had, his children would have a better life than he did.

And he was right.

My dad, Hugh, made it to college. He played football at Penn State and enlisted in the Navy after Pearl Harbor.

When the war was over he started his own small business, printing fabric for draperies.

I remember watching him stand for hours over silk screens.

He wanted to give my brothers and me opportunities he never had.

And he did. My mother, Dorothy, was abandoned by her parents as a young girl. She ended up on her own at 14, working as a house maid.

She was saved by the kindness of others.

Her first grade teacher saw she had nothing to eat at lunch, and brought extra food to share.

The lesson she passed on to me years later stuck with me:

No one gets through life alone.

We have to look out for each other and lift each other up.

She made sure I learned the words of our Methodist faith:

"Do all the good you can, for all the people you can, in all the ways you can, as long as ever you can."

I went to work for the Children's Defense Fund, going door-to-door in New Bedford, Massachusetts on behalf of children with disabilities who were denied the chance to go to school.

I remember meeting a young girl in a wheelchair on the small back porch of her house.

She told me how badly she wanted to go to school — it just didn't seem possible.

And I couldn't stop thinking of my mother and what she went through as a child.

It became clear to me that simply caring is not enough.

To drive real progress, you have to change both hearts and laws.

You need both understanding and action.

So we gathered facts. We built a coalition. And our work helped convince Congress to ensure access to education for all students with disabilities.

It's a big idea, isn't it?

Every kid with a disability has the right to go to school.

But how do you make an idea like that real? You do it step-by-step, year-by-year ... sometimes even door-by-door.

And my heart just swelled when I saw Anastasia Somoza on this stage, representing millions of young people who — because of those changes to our laws — are able to get an education.

It's true ... I sweat the details of policy — whether we're talking about the exact level of lead in the drinking water in Flint, Michigan, the number of mental health facilities in Iowa, or the cost of your prescription drugs.

Because it's not just a detail if it's your kid — if it's your family.

It's a big deal. And it should be a big deal to your president.

Over the last three days, you've seen some of the people who've inspired me.

People who let me into their lives, and became a part of mine.

People like Ryan Moore and Lauren Manning.

They told their stories Tuesday night.

I first met Ryan as a seven-year old.

He was wearing a full body brace that must have weighed forty pounds.

Children like Ryan kept me going when our plan for universal health care failed ... and kept me working with leaders of both parties to help create the Children's Health Insurance Program that covers 8 million kids every year.

It was the thought of her, and Debbie St. John, and John Dolan and Joe Sweeney, and all the victims and survivors, that kept me working as hard as I could in the Senate on behalf of 9/11 families, and our first responders who got sick from their time at Ground Zero.

I was still thinking of Lauren, Debbie and all the others ten years later in the White House Situation Room when President Obama made the courageous decision that finally brought Osama bin Laden to justice.

In this campaign, I've met so many people who motivate me to keep fighting for change.

And, with your help, I will carry all of your voices and stories with me to the White House.

I will be a President for Democrats, Republicans, and Independents.

For the struggling, the striving and the successful.

For those who vote for me and those who don't.

For all Americans.

Tonight, we've reached a milestone in our nation's march toward a more perfect union: the first time that a major party has nominated a woman for President.

Standing here as my mother's daughter, and my daughter's mother, I'm so happy this day has come.

Happy for grandmothers and little girls and everyone in between.

Happy for boys and men, too — because when any barrier falls in America, for anyone, it clears the way for everyone. When there are no ceilings, the sky's the limit.

So let's keep going, until every one of the 161 million women and girls across America has the opportunity she deserves.

Because even more important than the history we make tonight, is the history we will write together in the years ahead.

Let's begin with what we're going to do to help working people in our country get ahead and stay ahead.

Now, I don't think President Obama and Vice President Biden get the credit they deserve for saving us from the worst economic crisis of our lifetimes.

Our economy is so much stronger than when they took office. Nearly 15 million new private-sector jobs. Twenty million more Americans with health insurance. And an auto industry that just had its best year ever. That's real progress.

But none of us can be satisfied with the status quo. Not by a long shot.

We're still facing deep-seated problems that developed long before the recession and have stayed with us through the recovery.

I've gone around our country talking to working families. And I've heard from so many of you who feel like the economy just isn't working.

Some of you are frustrated — even furious.

And you know what? You're right.

It's not yet working the way it should.

Americans are willing to work — and work hard.

But right now, an awful lot of people feel there is less and less respect for the work they do.

And less respect for them, period.

Democrats are the party of working people.

But we haven't done a good enough job showing that we get what you're going through, and that we're going to do something about it.

So I want to tell you tonight how we will empower Americans to live better lives.

My primary mission as President will be to create more opportunity and more good jobs with rising wages right here in the United States.

From my first day in office to my last!

Especially in places that for too long have been left out and left behind.

From our inner cities to our small towns, from Indian Country to Coal Country.

From communities ravaged by addiction to regions hollowed out by plant closures.

And here's what I believe.

I believe America thrives when the middle class thrives.

I believe that our economy isn't working the way it should because our democracy isn't working the way it should.

That's why we need to appoint Supreme Court justices who will get money out of politics and expand voting rights, not restrict them. And we'll pass a constitutional amendment to overturn Citizens United!

I believe American corporations that have gotten so much from our country should be just as patriotic in return.

Many of them are. But too many aren't.

It's wrong to take tax breaks with one hand and give out pink slips with the other.

And I believe Wall Street can never, ever be allowed to wreck Main Street again.

I believe in science. I believe that climate change is real and that we can save our planet while creating millions of good-paying clean energy jobs.

I believe that when we have millions of hardworking immigrants contributing to our economy, it would be self-defeating and inhumane to kick them out.

Comprehensive immigration reform will grow our economy and keep families together — and it's the right thing to do.

Whatever party you belong to, or if you belong to no party at all, if you share these beliefs, this is your campaign.

If you believe that companies should share profits with their workers, not pad executive bonuses, join us.

If you believe the minimum wage should be a living wage ... and no one working full time should have to raise their children in poverty ... join us.

If you believe that every man, woman, and child in America has the right to affordable health care ... join us.

If you believe that we should say "no" to unfair trade deals ... that we should stand up to China ... that we should support our steelworkers and autoworkers and homegrown manufacturers ... join us.

If you believe we should expand Social Security and protect a woman's right to make her own health care decisions ... join us.

And yes, if you believe that your working mother, wife, sister, or daughter deserves equal pay ... join us.

Let's make sure this economy works for everyone, not just those at the top.

Now, you didn't hear any of this from Donald Trump at his convention.

He spoke for 70-odd minutes — and I do mean odd.

And he offered zero solutions. But we already know he doesn't believe these things.

No wonder he doesn't like talking about his plans.

You might have noticed, I love talking about mine.

In my first 100 days, we will work with both parties to pass the biggest investment in new, good-paying jobs since World War II.

Jobs in manufacturing, clean energy, technology and innovation, small business, and infrastructure.

If we invest in infrastructure now, we'll not only create jobs today, but lay the foundation for the jobs of the future.

And we will transform the way we prepare our young people for those jobs.

Bernie Sanders and I will work together to make college tuition-free for the middle class and debt-free for all!

We will also liberate millions of people who already have student debt.

It's just not right that Donald Trump can ignore his debts, but students and families can't refinance theirs.

And here's something we don't say often enough: College is crucial, but a four-year degree should not be the only path to a good job.

We're going to help more people learn a skill or practice a trade and make a good living doing it.

We're going to give small businesses a boost. Make it easier to get credit. Way too many dreams die in the parking lots of banks.

In America, if you can dream it, you should be able to build it.

We're going to help you balance family and work. And you know what, if fighting for affordable child care and paid family leave is playing the "woman card," then Deal Me In!

(Oh, you've heard that one?)

Now, here's the thing, we're not only going to make all these investments, we're going to pay for every single one of them.

And here's how: Wall Street, corporations, and the super rich are going to start paying their fair share of taxes.

Not because we resent success. Because when more than 90 percent of the gains have gone to the top 1 percent, that's where the money is.

And if companies take tax breaks and then ship jobs overseas, we'll make them pay us back. And we'll put that money to work where it belongs ... creating jobs here at home!

Now I know some of you are sitting at home thinking, well that all sounds pretty good.

But how are you going to get it done? How are you going to break through the gridlock in Washington? Look at my record. I've worked across the aisle to pass laws and treaties and to launch new programs that help millions of people. And if you give me the chance, that's what I'll do as President.

But Trump, he's a businessman. He must know something about the economy.

Well, let's take a closer look.

In Atlantic City, 60 miles from here, you'll find contractors and small businesses who lost everything because Donald Trump refused to pay his bills.

People who did the work and needed the money, and didn't get it — not because he couldn't pay them, but because he wouldn't pay them.

That sales pitch he's making to be your president? Put your faith in him — and you'll win big? That's the same sales pitch he made to all those small businesses. Then Trump walked away, and left working people holding the bag.

He also talks a big game about putting America First. Please explain to me what part of America First leads him to make Trump ties in China, not Colorado.

Trump suits in Mexico, not Michigan. Trump furniture in Turkey, not Ohio. Trump picture frames in India, not Wisconsin.

Donald Trump says he wants to make America great again — well, he could start by actually making things in America again.

The choice we face is just as stark when it comes to our national security.

Anyone reading the news can see the threats and turbulence we face.

From Baghdad and Kabul, to Nice and Paris and Brussels, to San Bernardino and Orlando, we're dealing with determined enemies that must be defeated.

No wonder people are anxious and looking for reassurance. Looking for steady leadership.

You want a leader who understands we are stronger when we work with our allies around the world and care for our veterans here at home. Keeping our nation safe and honoring the people who do it will be my highest priority.

I'm proud that we put a lid on Iran's nuclear program without firing a single shot — now we have to enforce it, and keep supporting Israel's security.

I'm proud that we shaped a global climate agreement — now we have to hold every country accountable to their commitments, including ourselves.

I'm proud to stand by our allies in NATO against any threat they face, including from Russia.

I've laid out my strategy for defeating ISIS.

We will strike their sanctuaries from the air, and support local forces taking them out on the ground. We will surge our intelligence so that we detect and prevent attacks before they happen.

We will disrupt their efforts online to reach and radicalize young people in our country.

It won't be easy or quick, but make no mistake — we will prevail.

Now Donald Trump says, and this is a quote, "I know more about ISIS than the generals do."

No, Donald, you don't.

He thinks that he knows more than our military because he claimed our armed forces are "a disaster."

Well, I've had the privilege to work closely with our troops and our veterans for many years, including as a senator on the Armed Services Committee.

I know how wrong he is. Our military is a national treasure.

We entrust our commander-in-chief to make the hardest decisions our nation faces.

Decisions about war and peace. Life and death.

A president should respect the men and women who risk their lives to serve our country — including the sons of Tim Kaine and Mike Pence, both Marines.

Ask yourself: Does Donald Trump have the temperament to be Commander-in-Chief?

Donald Trump can't even handle the rough-and-tumble of a presidential campaign.

He loses his cool at the slightest provocation. When he's gotten a tough question from a reporter. When he's challenged in a debate. When he sees a protester at a rally.

Imagine him in the Oval Office facing a real crisis. A man you can bait with a tweet is not a man we can trust with nuclear weapons.

I can't put it any better than Jackie Kennedy did after the Cuban Missile Crisis. She said that what worried President Kennedy during that very dangerous time was that a war might be started — not by big men with self-control and restraint, but by little men — the ones moved by fear and pride.

America's strength doesn't come from lashing out.

Strength relies on smarts, judgment, cool resolve, and the precise and strategic application of power.

That's the kind of Commander-in-Chief I pledge to be.

And if we're serious about keeping our country safe, we also can't afford to have a President who's in the pocket of the gun lobby.

I'm not here to repeal the Second Amendment.

I'm not here to take away your guns.

I just don't want you to be shot by someone who shouldn't have a gun in the first place.

We should be working with responsible gun owners to pass common-sense reforms and keep guns out of the hands of criminals, terrorists and all others who would do us harm.

For decades, people have said this issue was too hard to solve and the politics were too hot to touch.

Sign Up for the First Draft Newsletter
Subscribe for updates on the White House and Congress, delivered to your inbox Monday through Friday.

But I ask you: How can we just stand by and do nothing?

You heard, you saw, family members of people killed by gun violence.

You heard, you saw, family members of police officers killed in the line of duty because they were outgunned by criminals.

I refuse to believe we can't find common ground here.

We have to heal the divides in our country.

Not just on guns. But on race. Immigration. And more.

That starts with listening to each other. Hearing each other. Trying, as best we can, to walk in each other's shoes.

So let's put ourselves in the shoes of young black and Latino men and women who face the effects of systemic racism, and are made to feel like their lives are disposable.

Let's put ourselves in the shoes of police officers, kissing their kids and spouses goodbye every day and heading off to do a dangerous and necessary job.

We will reform our criminal justice system from end-to-end, and rebuild trust between law enforcement and the communities they serve.

We will defend all our rights — civil rights, human rights and voting rights ... women's rights and workers' rights ... LGBT rights and the rights of people with disabilities!

And we will stand up against mean and divisive rhetoric wherever it comes from.

For the past year, many people made the mistake of laughing off Donald Trump's comments — excusing him as an entertainer just putting on a show.

They think he couldn't possibly mean all the horrible things he says — like when he called women "pigs." Or said that an American judge couldn't be fair because of his Mexican heritage. Or when he mocks and mimics a reporter with a disability.

Or insults prisoners of war like John McCain — a true hero and patriot who deserves our respect.

At first, I admit, I couldn't believe he meant it either.

It was just too hard to fathom — that someone who wants to lead our nation could say those things. Could be like that.

But here's the sad truth: There is no other Donald Trump ... This is it.

And in the end, it comes down to what Donald Trump doesn't get: that America is great — because America is good.

So enough with the bigotry and bombast. Donald Trump's not offering real change.

He's offering empty promises. What are we offering? A bold agenda to improve the lives of people across our country — to keep you safe, to get you good jobs, and to give your kids the opportunities they deserve.

The choice is clear.

Every generation of Americans has come together to make our country freer, fairer, and stronger.

None of us can do it alone.

I know that at a time when so much seems to be pulling us apart, it can be hard to imagine how we'll ever pull together again.

But I'm here to tell you tonight — progress is possible.

I know because I've seen it in the lives of people across America who get knocked down and get right back up.

And I know it from my own life. More than a few times, I've had to pick myself up and get back in the game.

Like so much else, I got this from my mother. She never let me back down from any challenge. When I tried to hide from a neighborhood bully, she literally blocked the door. "Go back out there," she said.

And she was right. You have to stand up to bullies.

You have to keep working to make things better, even when the odds are long and the opposition is fierce.

We lost my mother a few years ago. I miss her every day. And I still hear her voice urging me to keep working, keep fighting for right, no matter what.

That's what we need to do together as a nation.

Though "we may not live to see the glory," as the song from the musical Hamilton goes, "let us gladly join the fight."

Let our legacy be about "planting seeds in a garden you never get to see."

That's why we're here … not just in this hall, but on this Earth.

The Founders showed us that.

And so have many others since.

They were drawn together by love of country, and the selfless passion to build something better for all who follow.

That is the story of America. And we begin a new chapter tonight.

Yes, the world is watching what we do.

Yes, America's destiny is ours to choose.

So let's be stronger together.

Looking to the future with courage and confidence.

Building a better tomorrow for our beloved children and our beloved country.

When we do, America will be greater than ever.

Thank you and may God bless the United States of America!

CPSIA information can be obtained
at www.ICGtesting.com
Printed in the USA
LVHW061601030220
645679LV00039B/2033